HOW POLARIZED RELATIONSHIPS SAVE THE WORLD:

Uniting the Sexes Through Psychological and Hormonal Health

Asa Santiago

CONTENTS

Polarity Basics: Core Structure   156

Additional Notes   176

Overall Conclusion   217

Disclaimer

This book does not make direct statements about disease, nor is it intended to diagnose, treat, or cure any medical condition. Any references to medical, psychological, or neurological conditions are solely for educational purposes, drawn from Asa's personal experience and observations. Asa is not a licensed healthcare professional and is not providing medical advice. The content within this book is meant to offer insights and share hypotheses, not present medical or psychological conclusions as absolute facts. Asa's work is purely educational and does not substitute for professional advice, diagnosis, or treatment.

Acknowledgements

I want to first thank my mother Anita Santiago for being a light in a very dark place for me; without her, I would be lost. My sister Christiana for helping me with the Pass the Torch program web design. Brad Campbell pitched in with the editing of this book. Rich Colburn was a positive influence regarding my spirituality and to better understand how various people view religion. Jeff Spicer for his intuitive and custom insights into business planning. Katrina & Roger Mattei helped me to better define the Developmental Archetypes through their example, and were very hospitable to me as I worked as a practitioner at The Vine Health and Wellness Center in Moscow, Idaho. Mark Cuda and Roman Massey at The Innovation Collective in Coeur d'Alene, Idaho were very supportive of my push forward as an entrepreneur. Roman felt a book would be important and timely. Travis Johnson, owner of Northwest Survival School, was instrumental in helping me to integrate more masculinity and become an overall more dynamic man. Bob Mero for helping me better understand masculinity at its peak. Brian Kuenning has been a great support for various projects in and out of the project, and I really appreciate his friendship. Geraecka Lyonns helped me to edit the majority of this book and has been a solid connection in my life overall.

There are many more people to mention, but I wanted to highlight those who really contributed to this writing specifically.

Dedication

This woman changed my life, and is a big part of the reason how I'm able to bring this book to the world. So, I dedicate this book to you, Ana.

Ana Gefvert was truly an enigma of a human being, and really the only person I ever felt was more fringe than me in the pursuit of reclaiming bodily health, haha...

She put herself in a position to travel freely, to deeply pursue healing, and to seek God's light after having cured her autism and several other serious illnesses by eating raw meat and fat. She explored the 'raw milk cure' as well.

We met back in 2018 when I first started the carnivore diet my vegan sister suggested I try. At the time I was more raw paleo. I was at Grocery Outlet grabbing up last of the cheap NY steaks, and there behind me was this sweet woman waiting for me to finish. I turned to her and said "oh hey...uhhh...yeah I'm on this carnivore diet, you can have some of the steak, here." She responded with "oh thank you, how nice. I'm a carnivore too! But I eat it raw!"

WHOA! What?! When I heard that, I said to myself 'no way, I thought I was the Steve O of alternative health pursuits.' So I offered to buy her the steak she was holding. She then invited me to go to one of her house sitting gigs watching some dogs.

She always gave the dogs the raw meat and the families couldn't figure out why their pets would have such a strong preference for her. At the place she took me to, she had me try a piece of raw rib suet while standing outside. She told me to look into the sun and perform what is called 'sun gazing' (this was in the middle of the day). So I took a bite of the fat while looking into the light and WOW did I have a hit of euphoria like no other. I felt my cells tingle and my heart warm. I came to life, and couldn't stop smiling; we both kept smiling into the sunlight...

If you think about it, the huge sum of people I've helped over the years may not have received that help without Ana. I have no idea how long it may have taken me to go online with my knowledge and the level of what knowledge I'd be missing without her example. Without the dry fasting she introduced me to, I may have never become masculine and would have likely been destined for sexual deviance and a pleasure-focused life.

She had been vegetarian for 20 or so years, around 10 vegan with some years raw if I remember correctly. Her hair apparently thinned out entirely, went grey, she looked emaciated, and was highly autistic with a lot of mold and mercury toxicity. A few months into the raw meat diet her hair recolored and grew back.

Hearing her story really impassioned me to enter the plant-based vs. carnivore debate. I really didn't want others to mistakenly end up on that road that can take 30 years to form.

So I really owe a lot to this woman. Ana was a true fighter. She knew what it was like to be that person at the most extreme lows of health. She uniquely knew what it was like to do the impossible and cure what is claimed cannot be cured. She really knew how to give and love while barely keeping her head above water.

Losing her last year was devastating. I wish she had listened to me, but a big part of why she wasn't listening was the same reason she managed to pull herself out of a dark hole. I'm sorry I didn't reach out more; I knew you were alone despite your strong independence; I'm sorry you left here alone. I feel that you wanted to go, that you were ready and that God was right there with you. I just wasn't ready, Ana. I love you.

I am so thankful for your wisdom and kindness Ana. I'm going to take the torch to the finish line. I hope you'll be there for it.

Introduction

The term 'polarity,' a term in the dating world symbolizing the masculine and feminine as units of polarity, became a big part of my life when I reached new stages of health. In my latter teens and then into my twenties, I had no understanding that my bodily chemistry could determine the outcome of my entire identity. That my 'metrosexual' personality, which once only found powerful women attractive—as I was in complete submission to them—wasn't actually who I was supposed to be.

My name is Asa Santiago, and while I would have preferred to become an entertainer in Hollywood years ago, I was propelled into alternative health sciences, both to survive and to align with my purpose to guide people to truths and a more optimal well-being.

Frustrated by the temporary solutions offered by professionals around me, I took the initiative to deeply explore and address my own health issues. This journey allowed me to find a stable foundation, enabling me to function effectively in both my personal and professional life. ADD/ADHD, clinical depression, chronic anxiety, skin problems, frequent joint pain, minor dyslexia, general gastrointestinal distress, frequently getting sick throughout the year, antibiotic damage, diagnosed vaccine injuries, and adverse sexual fantasies were a big part of my identity in my past.

In this book, I will share the basics of what a polarized masculine man and feminine woman really should look like through a lens of personal experience, scientific evidence that exists, and experimentation. I've devoted a couple thousand hours of research seeking to fit together the pieces of a vastly complex puzzle that made up the hormonal challenges I had faced. I've lived both as a masculine man courting feminine women, and, earlier, as a man in a more submissive role to women. Without these experiences, I wouldn't have the ability to write this book. Through personal experience and intuition, together with a vast understanding of human psychology and biology, understanding polarized relationships now comes far more easily.

Being born into illness and experiencing the subsequent challenges and pitfalls, I sought answers through, in part, the study of nutrition, neurology, endocrinology, and epidemiology for over 9 years. This came on the heels of my two years of sporadic college education to become a Natural Doctor. I dropped out after realizing that even the natural side of things can be encumbered by the rule of centralized institutions. I formed the company Polarity Health LLC in early 2024 after dissolving Gut Goals LLC, through which I offered free and small cost advice to online groups for 4 years. My role now is to be a health educator, health and relationships coach, and health consultant, utilizing functional medicine for people as a practitioner, not as a doctor.

The full story of how I came to be masculine through many hardships will be revealed in a separate book. The main purpose of this book is meant to describe the basics of polarity from a different lens.

MY STORY & CAREER IN BRIEF

My mother came from a generation that wasn't really aware that margarine is a far worse alternative than butter, that antibiotics are good and have negligible contraindications, that vaccines are humanity's savior, that the immune system isn't capable without medical insights and interventions, that believing dental procedures like dental amalgams with 'silver fillings' were necessary, that they are made entirely of silver (they weren't), and that mercury from those amalgams cannot harm or leak and accumulate in her system and eventually her placenta...

I hold no blame for the professionals who led my mother to believe these lies, nor would I ever blame her. However, the people who created the curriculum the professionals learned from, and the people in business who benefit from the medical, dental, and food industries, can absolutely be held accountable for the fallout of the generations affected by the side effects of consumers using their services and products. I am a part of that generation, and many of the readers may be as well.

The indirect effects of many antibiotics, vaccines, some dental surgeries, poor diet (including portion size, even if the quality is good), and environmental toxins can definitely be passed on to a child from both the mother and father. This, I'm sure, has caused profound and irreparable harm to global physical and mental health.

While I may have my issues, having been born with a systemic Candida albicans infection and an abnormal amount of what is called 'cradle cap' (potentially connected to a fungus named malassezia), many other children had it much worse, or just different—the dice roll of life our modern world provides.

The Beginning

By the age of two I was on antifungal medication for systemic candida, which eventually subsided and was presumed to be healed. Life went on in normal fashion until the age of 3 ½, when a friend of my mother's highly recommended the local preschool her boys attended for socialization and learning 2-3 half days per week. My mom thought it was a good idea since I didn't get much exposure to kids my age, having had only my younger baby sister around.

After a couple of months passed and while visiting family up north, my mother had a sudden jolting premonition of my teenage cousin, Jon, dying while she hugged him goodbye. She then pleaded with my father to take him back with them once Jon was out of earshot. After a desperate and emotional back and forth, my father became frustrated, saying it was crazy, not to mention impossible to take him out of school, given the 3 hour distance of our home. She eventually relented and the devastating call came two weeks later that Jon was hit and killed by a train.

[*Later in the book I go over the importance of 'feminine intuition,' and how a woman's abilities shouldn't be discounted.*]

About a month after the funeral when I was back in preschool, my mother had a gut feeling to pull me out. She asked me questions about it but nothing surfaced. As she reflects now, she noticed my smile in subsequent months didn't look the same. During that time there was much tumult, between the beginning of my parents' divorce and PTSD coming to roost for my mom during the funeral surfacing an old trauma. She thought it had to do with my being affected by the emotional emotional strain of those around me.

But by the age of 5, I was having partial dreams of a white-haired older woman locking me in cages. Some partial dreams and fantasies were much more sexual, something a 5 year old isn't going to dream up at random. By the age of 12, I was expressing to my mom the kind of dreams and partial fantasies I was having. She asked details about where I was and what this person looked like in the dreams. After more details surfaced, the more clear it became - It was partial memories tied to the older woman who ran the preschool. She spoke then about how maybe something happened there when I was little. We talked further and decided to get help for it and my deepening depression.

Therapy and a good diet with supplementation helped, but the things I had become interested in lingered. I had no ability to fight off the urges; even becoming somewhat obsessed. Around the age of 10, I had cut my father off due to witnessing him doing some things to other people that were cruel.

After experiencing a mix of good moments, depression, anxiety, and missed opportunities due to a father wound, I landed a job at Starbucks at age 18. This was a high point for me, because my life otherwise felt directionless while focused on playing video games and escaping internal pain. I did not do well for the first 6 months due to the attention deficit disorder (ADD/ADHD, and yes I know they changed it to ADHD, but I still personally see them as separate in my case) I was diagnosed with. But then eventually became Partner of the Quarter across the district, and the first to be given the Coffee Master title by a tenured district manager in Marin County, CA.

[ADD/ADHD, in simple terms, can be characterized by a persistent difficulty in maintaining focus and attention, often due to altered dopamine regulation in the brain. This leads to a constant search for stimulation or novelty to fulfill the brain's need for dopamine, contributing to frequent distraction and difficulty with sustained effort.]

I excelled at the job and worked well with customers, but I struggled to navigate the social gray areas between following corporate standards and those who didn't. My former coworkers might find it hard to believe that I now stand against "the system." Back then, I was confidently telling everyone I would be come the President of the United States, all while holding myself in celibacy for one woman I would fall in love with some day.

I eventually moved to Tahoe at the age of 21 with my family, became the local college mascot, got a job in a restaurant, met the girl of my dreams there, and eventually hit a point of heartbreak, because she and I were like oil and water. It wasn't due to chemical incompatibility, but because she was deeply immersed in the "living wild" scene— doing lines, engaging in orgies, and living a high-adrenaline lifestyle. I was very much still like I was at Starbucks, staunch about doing the right thing and staying clean, so I directly told her what she was doing wasn't good for her. After weeks of phone silence, I had the notion that maybe learning the entire Napoleon Dynamite dance just might impress her, or at least bring a smile to her face. But the opportunity to show her never came, as she flatly rejected me. I was so distraught I ended up performing the dance to a bar crowd, and soon after hit rock bottom and had a panic attack.

When the age of 22 rolled around, I looked at my skin and overall health and told myself that I won't get women until my body gets better. I began trying to address the chicken scratch marks on my arms and eventually narrowed it down to a potential cause: Candida, the systemic yeast I was born with.

Within two weeks of cleansing my gut of fungus, I lost the joint pain, skin issues, chronic anxiety, clinical depression, and stopped getting sick. Once I felt better, I never looked back; adopting an entirely organic paleo-centric diet and spending time at the gym. I became much more confident, so much so that I would dance on treadmills publicly.

At some point, I completely ruined my celibacy streak because I told myself it was making me chronically under-confident; that women want experienced men. I navigated a series of experiences during that time, and unfortunately, I hurt a few girls. I struggled with conflicting sexual thoughts, which often left me unable to maintain arousal during intimate moments. I would go flaccid pretty quickly and this was obviously not the goal. I now, however, recognize that I would only do this with the more masculine presenting women, but not the more feminine women *(a key insight to remember for this book)*. The masculine presenting women had to take charge and be sexually dominant in order for me to find them attractive.

By the age of 24, I moved back to the Bay Area and engaged in profound self-discovery while eating the same way organically. I dated several attractive women and experienced a bit of a spiral when one relationship didn't work out. In search of a new path, I ventured into the kink scene in the city, hoping to find a dominant partner to serve. Remarkably, at my very first event, I encountered a powerful woman with whom I felt a profound connection.

This relationship went on for several fun, intense, but emotionally harrowing months where blood, sweat, and tears were a literal reality. I signed an NDA (non-disclosure agreement) before we separated, and I ended up with another dominant woman right after that who was a genuine girlfriend rather than the contractual previous experience. At that time, I didn't realize her copper IUD and mild autism were significant factors influencing her strong desire to dominate me in specific ways. I believe the autism also contributed to her connection to a deity she dreamt of that was apparently telling her to do these sexually sadistic (sexual sadism is a desire to inflict pain) things to me. We eventually separated when I took a bite of raw meat when trying a raw paleo diet *(I had hit a wall with my current cooked paleo diet, so I did a random experiment by going all raw. The first raw meat meal almost completely wiped out my desires for BDSM-related sex).*

Eventually, my sister suggested I try the new trending carnivore diet. I don't normally follow trends, but it made sense to me because opportunistic microbes need sugar to grow, so such a diet would suppress them on a profound level. Upon entering the carnivore online universe, I found it odd to discover they were focused on plant toxins, which is far from the reason why the carnivore diet is so beneficial for autoimmunity, in my opinion. I had even written a professional article for a medical doctor on oxalates, the most potent plant toxin that is said to mostly be acquired from food, that we know of today.

Before my involvement in the carnivore diet world online, I met a gal named Ana Gefvert in a grocery store. Ana–the person I've dedicated this book to–shared her remarkable story of curing most of her autism, mercury poisoning, fraying and grayed hair, and several other big wins by eating only raw meat and nothing else. Ana said she was vegan for 10 years, and vegetarian for longer. She was the one who inspired me to join Facebook and check out the raw carnivore group that I've since convinced the group admins to rename it as "*Carnivores Gone Raw.*" Yeah, I try to be funny where I can; we even made Smeagle from Lord of the Rings our mascot.

I did a lot of experiments, including trying more raw meat and suet with Ana, and wow was that an experience. Similar to my first awakening trying raw meat with my ex, and temporarily losing my desires for sexual violence done to me, I had, what I would call, a hugely blissful holy affect trying the raw fat with Ana while she taught me sungazing. Looking up into the 12pm sun drew an automatic smile on my face.

Ana also told me about 'dry fasting,' which was probably the biggest thing she could have shown me for better health. Dry fasting *(dry fasting is a process where one doesn't consume water or food for a period of time)* has changed my life, and was the largest trigger for my masculinization today.

Flash forward to my journey way north, where I found myself at Northwest Survival School , owned and operated by Travis Johnson —a supremely accomplished survivalist who at 17 ventured high into the North Cascades alone for a year with nothing more than two wool blankets and a knife. Under Travis' guidance, training and many hardcore experiences in the remote wilderness for three years, I was able to reach a pivotal place in my quest to fill the void left by an unrealized father wound. By integrating masculine competency at the school participating in and being instrumental in training others I was able to reclaim and embody a vital missing part of myself while operating my online health business, Gut Goals.

A couple of years later I headed back to winter in California at my mother's place. Soon thereafter I met a gal online and convinced her to come for a visit. Dating this girl was a different experience on a whole new level. Although her visit was brief, I experienced a sense of masculinity that I had never felt before in the presence of anyone else. She had very **receiving** energy, and when I slept next to her for the first time, I had a lucid dream. Maybe this isn't big for a lot of people, but I have never in my life fully remembered any dream, nor anything fully lucid.

Being with her, I also did a lot better at a job I picked up part-time to supplement my income. It was a lead generation gig for a gutter protection company. I completely killed it with my quota, consistently exceeding it.

Prior to having her visit, I had done a few experiments with my health and conducted my 17th 3-day consecutive dry fast. This was the most powerful one I had ever done; wherein other fasts gallstones, or caused growth of chest hair, and generally improved mental health–but nothing like this. After that fast, a good section of my beard went red, and a day after, I felt my blood surge with warmth.

I also felt a profound feeling and images pervaded my mind of all of the past experiences I had growing up being connected like they were meant to happen. It was this day I really started to believe that there is a God up there watching over me (you can believe what you want, this was my experience), giving me the means to heal wounds that society believed impossible to rectify.

Days after, I would enter grocery stores, see a woman I liked, and walk directly to them to get their number. I felt an incredible surge of confidence, attracting the attention of women who turned their heads in my direction, while also catching the interest of men who were eager to form friendships. Suffice it to say, I would get this kind of 'superpower' that I believed was testosterone, but it was actually much more than that.

Accompanying this newfound confidence was a significant suppression of any desire to be dominated by women. The solution I had long been searching for revealed itself to me as not being a complete cure, but rather a deep understanding of the underlying causes, akin to being in a state of remission. I came to recognize that my feelings of inferiority towards women, my admiration for a nurturing and capable mother figure, the absence of a father, and my perceived inability to provide were the core factors driving those desires. Though later in this book I explain in greater detail how my desires were influenced hormonally.

I experienced many adventures following that transition, with ups and downs and more self-discovery. I realized that the fast had not only made me feel more connected with a higher power, but things were manifesting much faster than before. Every high and low I experienced felt essential to the journey I felt destined to undertake, shaping everything I needed to reach this point today.

There was a moment, however, about a year ago that proved to me the existence of a dark force—a force that seeks to persuade me to say "yes" and dive headfirst back into the darkness. On a spiritual level, I believe something has been pulling at me my entire life, coaxing me to abandon my path of betterment and instead pursue self-focus and fleeting pleasure. This force, both seductive and destructive, has always lurked in the shadows, testing the strength of my resolve; also proving to me the fact that there is a God and an opposing evil. At that time the relationship I was in a the time was unraveling, leaving me in a low, vulnerable place. In that state, I found myself revisiting an old online account from the kink world. There were no messages, just an empty void of possibilities— an open door tempting me to sabotage myself and pursue those women. The pull toward destruction, disguised as opportunity, felt insidious yet familiar, a reminder of the ease with which one can slip into old patterns when the foundation of a relationship begins to crack.

Around that time I just so happened to be watching an anime where a little boy was an ambiguous consort to a money-driven woman with white long hair who was respected for her ability to slay demons. The image of she and him and the way she spoke to him was like a copy of my dynamic with my first Domme/Mistress. The whole look, the entire vibe, all strikingly reminiscent of the first instance of molestation I experienced.

Right as I was watching that scene in the anime, I took a screenshot and sent it to that first Domme who hadn't spoken to me in years. To my surprise, in the message area, it showed that she was typing a message to me before I did anything. Something unique about our connection that I can share was that she generally wouldn't engage with me unless I had her strongly in my mind—almost as if I was pulling her in energetically.

I've experienced similar things in past relationships. For instance, one of my exes once had a panic attack around the exact same time I was in distress and needed to speak with her. That was during a time when I was far more feminine and struggled deeply with relationships as a whole. I'm not sure but I have heard that when we have intimate relationships a thick unseen bond is created which allows for this connection or pull. My first Domme found this curious and would call me "gypsy boy"... Interestingly, I have some Czech Gypsy heritage.

In her message, before knowing I was going to send something, she offered to see me again and potentially revive what we had. I said no right off, and that I need to realize who I am meant to be; that I cannot be that man living within a cycle of debauchery and pleasure.

Despite my yearning for her all those years prior to the prior to the fast? I think you need to expand on this. Maybe this: prior to the health leaps, fasting and training, even in a very weak moment, I said no.

Either way, the dry fast I had done years ago did cure me of much of the desire behind the affiar/dynamic *(I actually tried multiple times to like it with women in person)*, but neurologically some of it lived for reasons relating to lack of fulfillment *(no girlfriend, no father figure)*.

What I hadn't realized was that there was still mercury in my system, despite all of the gut cleansing and extreme dieting. The ADD - likely caused by the mercury and some other factors - would recurrently cause me to have deficits in competency and lead me toward the mental states that would cause me to think of these women.

Moving more of the mercury out as my ex and I were separating was the big one, the way for me to - even when perceiving failure with women - still have no desire to be dominated by them. I believe the surge in testosterone that came from the suppressed ADD, among a few other big factors anatomically, was all I needed to finally never look back.

Now in 2025, I've guided hundreds of people to help themselves and progress their own health, so as not to be reliant on the system. I've been on several podcasts, spoken at corporate events, and taught training seminars to a variety of professionals. I've educated psychologists, natural doctors, med students, medical doctors, business professionals, and various PhDs on my view of functional medicine, developmental psychology, and systems biology.

Career & Asa's Scientific Views and Theories

It's first important to understand the framework of how I think so the reader can really follow along.

Unlicensed naturopathic functional medicine has widely been my field of expertise since late 2018 (meaning I don't treat, diagnose, or make direct claims about someone's disease or medical condition due to being unlicensed, but focusing on full-body wellness). After getting certified in functional nutrition, I took a particular angle toward what is called 'systems biology.' Systems biology would see something like endocrine disruption (endocrinology is the study of hormones) as a 'disturbance,' and the liver as an integral part of the endocrine system. Functional work is altogether more focused on the root cause, which would primarily be disturbances to the system.

A simple way to understand systems science is by recognizing that nearly everything around us is a system, where some systems are more or less intelligent than others. Many biological systems will have basic functions like an 'input,' 'output,' 'transport,' 'controller,' and 'goal.' Our most major focus here is the human body, where we may consider the controller for the endocrine system as the hypothalamus or pituitary gland.

To explain better the roles of a 'system' specific to hormones, here are the components:

Input: The input to the endocrine system consists of various signals or stimuli that trigger hormonal responses. These inputs can include environmental cues (such as light, temperature, or stress), physiological signals (such as nutrient levels or blood pressure), neural signals (from the nervous system), or feedback signals from other endocrine glands or organs.

Output: The output of the endocrine system is the secretion of hormones into the bloodstream by endocrine glands. These hormones act as chemical messengers, traveling through the bloodstream to target tissues or organs where they exert their effects. The output of the endocrine system can also include physiological responses or changes in target tissues in response to hormone action.

Controller: The controller of the endocrine system involves various regulatory mechanisms that coordinate hormone secretion and maintain homeostasis. These include feedback loops involving hormone levels, neural inputs from the hypothalamus and pituitary gland (often referred to as the "master gland"), and other control mechanisms that adjust hormone production in response to internal or external cues.

Transport: The transport component of the endocrine system involves the movement of hormones through the bloodstream to reach target tissues or organs. Hormones are released into the bloodstream by endocrine glands, travel to distant target cells or organs, and bind to specific receptors to initiate cellular responses. Blood circulation serves as the primary mode of transport for hormones in the body.

Goal: The goal of the endocrine system is to regulate various physiological processes and maintain homeostasis within the body. This includes regulating metabolism, growth and development, reproduction, stress response, immune function, and many other functions. The overall goal is to ensure that the body's internal environment remains stable and conducive to optimal health and functioning.

There is no need to remember all of this, but it is important to establish somewhat of a framework in the reader's mind in order to get an idea of what I'm presenting as a broader argument as it pertains to polarity in this book.

Theory of Disease

Something important to know is that while many coaches and practitioners utilize systems science and focus on root causes, very few of them have the same exact views on the root cause, let alone agree on the solution. Generally, there isn't much science stating absolutes. There are still wars over Germ Theory and Terrain Theory, and my own views differ from both, hence I created what I call the Opportunism Theory of disease.

The Terrain Theory perspective: When the human body (the terrain) hits a poor state of health, imbalances occur where microbes come to clean up the toxins. Aajonus Vonderplanitz is a big proponent of this viewpoint, and while I respect his other work, I do not agree that microbes generally only clean up decaying flesh and toxins. Some in Terrain Theory do believe the imbalance leads to microbes becoming opportunistic. However, they primarily don't believe in rectifying the imbalance by going after the microbes that appear from such an imbalance. It is also a common belief that viruses either don't exist or have no association with disease whatsoever.

The Germ Theory perspective: Microbial viruses, bacteria/archaea, fungi (yeast/mold/dermatophytes), and parasites (helminth/protozoa/ectoparasites) all have the capacity to cause or lead to disease at any given time, whether the host has poor health or not. This perspective is what the mainstream believes as a whole and is what drives the pharmaceutical industry. Antibiotics and vaccination are common modalities in medical care regarding this theory.

The Opportunism Theory perspective: In short, when someone chooses to live outside of the human blueprint, they make themselves susceptible to microbes seeking new territory in their bodies. This is a merit-based perspective. Only living microbes have the capacity to opportunistically seek more than what they are given in the host (you) ecosystem, which can result in disease over a period of time within a weak or strong host; the strength of the host determines the level of opportunism. This theory also questions why intracellular (inside of the cell) viruses are seen as more pathogenic than extracellular (outside of the cell) viruses, aka 'phages.'

It's important to remember that these perspectives still remain theories in early 2025. I do not stand with my theory as if it is absolute fact, but I feel it is the most logical to date.

Original Works

I am an experimentalist of my own body and have uncovered modalities that, to my knowledge, have yet to reach mainstream recognition. For example, I have discovered that dry fasting can remove gallstones, mitigate trauma, balance minerals, eliminate heavy metals, and adapt the epigenetic host state to better align with its environment for survival.

Early in my career, I emphasized that the carnivore diet is not merely about avoiding "plant toxins" but also about targeting eukaryotic opportunistic microbes, such as fungi and parasites, which rely on sugar and glucose to thrive and expand. This perspective only became mainstream years later. Similarly, I have argued against the concept of "vitamin A toxicity," as proposed by some health professionals who claim that vitamin A is inherently toxic. Instead, I believe this issue stems from excess stored retinyl esters and a lack of fasting, which is necessary to activate stem cells and rebalance the system.

I have also hypothesized that endometriosis may arise from women frequently oscillating between fight-or-flight responses. Chronic stress diverts pregnenolone—essential for progesterone production, which balances estrogen—toward cortisol production instead. This imbalance could lead to the formation of endometrial tissue outside the uterus. Cortisol, as the primary glucocorticoid hormone, supports critical bodily functions during stress. Literature, such as the study referenced under PMID: 32046437, has drawn connections between chronic stress and endometriosis.

Additionally, I have observed a strong correlation between father or masculine wounds—or circumstances in which women are forced into survival mode—and the development of PCOS. While the exact biochemical causes remain uncertain, I suspect Candida and Small Intestinal Fungal Overgrowth (SIFO) play a significant role. Anecdotal evidence suggests that antifungal treatments have helped women with PCOS, indicating that Candida, as an opportunistic organism, may be linked to emotional imbalances. The sugar cravings often associated with fungal infections can drive excess insulin production, contributing to PCOS and its characteristic insulin resistance. Many believe insulin resistance is a primary issue, as a carnivore diet has been shown to reduce the small, fluid-filled ovarian cysts seen in some women. Furthermore, I propose that similar microbial imbalances, like Candida overgrowth, may underlie prostate health issues, as numerous men have reported improvements after addressing fungi and parasites in their gut.

In my own health journey, I discovered a potential connection between Attention Deficit Disorder (ADD/ADHD) and an excess of femininity, while Autism Spectrum Disorder (ASD) seems to correlate with an excess of masculinity. As you read this book, these hallmark traits may become more apparent. In the chapter titled Proposed

Hypothesis and Perspective - Psychology, there is a section called ADD/ADHD & ASD, where I delve into the theory that ADD and ASD reflect feminine and masculine imbalances, respectively. Don't worry—I am not being literal by referring to these conditions as creatures of fantasy.

Finally, I have developed a process that combines peer-to-peer counseling and health coaching techniques to help individuals realign their sexual attractions with their authentic blueprint. This approach began when a highly educated, married lesbian doctor contacted me after hearing me on a podcast. Following a few in-depth conversations, she eventually transitioned into a heterosexual relationship with a man.

*It's important to disclaim that **I do not perform conversion therapy.** My approach is focused on guiding individuals to uncover answers within themselves. My work is a process of liberating someone from falsehoods and aiding them in reconnecting with their authentic self. Through developing systems to facilitate this transformation, I created the "Developmental Archetypes," which I will elaborate on further in the book.*

Concluding Asa's Story & Career

Much has come from this long, unconventional journey I've been on. Some of the first individuals who came to me were at their breaking point, struggling to survive. Many of you may not have witnessed the drastic effects of certain medications, such as Ciprofloxacin, where a healthy, athletic person can quickly give the impression of being reduced to just skin and bones.

Often, I find myself doing everything I can to help others who feel overwhelmed by their circumstances, supporting them in their quest for hope and healing. My work is centered on exploring new modalities to assist those in distress, but it is essential to clarify that I do not provide medical advice or therapy.

I now have the torch in my hand, and am aiming to get it to the finish line. That finish line is to the readers here, and anyone they share this book with. My hope is that this book will serve as a resource for individuals to either embark on their journey or continue progressing from their current point. It is designed to help each reach their best selves while fostering and maintaining meaningful polarized relationships. And yes, I believe a great majority of us can polarize.

Objections that I've encountered to this statement will be discussed in the "Common Objections" section of the book.

Stay tuned for the future release of the book dedicated solely to my story. These are my handles to stay updated:

Facebook/Instagram: @AsaSantiago

X: @AsaSantiag0 ← that's a zero

LinkedIn: https://www.linkedin.com/in/asa-santiago/

Website: https://www.Polarizinghealth.com

Youtube: @AsaSantiago

DEFINING POLARITY

Polarity, in a relationship sense, primarily focuses strongly on the individual traits of a masculine man and a feminine woman from a more philosophical–and at times, spiritual and esoteric– perspective. When I entered the scene, I quickly realized that people weren't connecting this back to any science or concrete evidence; that it's not just an idea or trend, but an immutable law of nature, when it comes to mankind.

It is important to know that I pull my view of polarity on the basis of optimal survival parameters, and assuming that not much has changed since the beginnings of mankind.

Loose Terms and Definitions

The following are terms I use when discussing the topic of polarity with members of my groups and clients.

Raw Femininity

Outside of scientific descriptions brought up later in the book, femininity in its most raw form is a kind of childlikeness. The child embodies creativity, openness, playfulness, love, compassion, and empathy, thriving in connection and emotional expression rather than strict logic. She lives in the moment, guided by intuition and sensitivity, bringing warmth and joy to her surroundings. Her focus is on relationships, connection, and understanding, viewing the world through a lens of curiosity and wonder. The childlike feminine nurtures without judgment, embraces spontaneity, and finds beauty in the simple pleasures of life, adding color and depth to those around her.

Raw Masculinity

The masculine in its most raw form is the adult. The adult is disciplined, structured, pragmatic, rational, and logical, embodying stability and consistency. He takes responsibility for himself and those around him, creating order and setting boundaries that foster growth and security. He values action and the mission over idle talk, always seeking to solve problems and overcome challenges with a steady hand, and so on...

So far, I have generally been sticking to referring to women at their peak of health and fulfillment as the *'radiant feminine,'* and men the *'emanating masculine.'*

Radiant Feminine

The radiant feminine woman enters the room with a glowing warmth people can feel. She is by and large loved and cherished by both men and women. She is loved and cherished by men and women.

A radiant woman has overcome 'female solipsism' to some extent, and isn't in a survival state of fight-or-flight on a regular basis. She is content, loved, and protected. From this position, she can focus on expression and creativity. Female solipsism is the tendency to interpret reality primarily through personal emotions and experiences, often prioritizing relational dynamics and subjective perspectives over objective facts.

She is well-versed in people, and seeks to understand all. She is able to peer into the most wounded and obstinate person, and see who they were before harm. Some radiant women have developed the ability to breathe life into such a person. Her love of people is followed by her optimistic thoughts of them, where she keeps a fairly clear mind oriented toward seeing the good in others.

She has grace, poise, and an overall ability to hold herself with a glowing outward presence; where her physical health ensures the glow stays strong.

She is engaging socially and very much present in the moment. She is a great listener and has a focus on winning hearts over.

This woman knows **why** she is here, and by effect, instills **purpose** in her children, while inspiring those within her surrounding tribe.

Emanating Masculine

The emanating masculine man steps into the room with a grounded intensity; people feel the strength of his presence, an energy that emanates stability and assurance, drawing respect from men, and admiration from women.

An emanating man has transcended self-centered ambitions and reactive aggression. He is at peace within himself, fully anchored and secure in his role. From this position, he can focus on leadership and creation, rather than mere survival.

He is a master of his domain, focused on creating order and achieving goals with precision and determination. His attention is fixed on actions and outcomes, seeking paths that drive progress and elevate those around him through his example. The emanating man possesses a rare ability to bring out the strength and discipline in others, challenging them to step into their potential through shared goals and constructive action.

He exudes control, strength, and an unwavering sense of purpose, carrying himself with a powerful yet calm presence, a reflection of his mastery over mind and body.

He moves through social spaces with intentionality and focus, drawing people in with his silent command. He speaks sparingly but with conviction, his words holding weight and purpose, and he draws loyalty by leading others toward a vision.

This man knows **what** he is here to build and protect, and by embodying this purpose, he instills vision in his children and galvanizes those within his community, empowering them to strive toward their own paths with courage and integrity. He teaches those around him how to complete the **mission** required to reach the purpose he and his people share.

Boy

When I utilize this word, I'm referring to the feminine within a man that makes him a child with underdeveloped masculine/adult qualities.

Masculinity can also be seen as the inner adult, and 'the father within.'

Girl

When I'm referring to a grown woman as a girl, she would be someone who has underdeveloped masculine/adult qualities.

The Father Within

This term represents what the father figure is supposed to provide a child during upbringing. Most people do not have a father who is an 'emanating masculine' figure in their lives. Not due to lack of trying, but that the world is so full of toxins that their testosterone is in some ways going to be undermined; this doesn't even get into all of the traps available to a man in modern society to become lesser.

The father prepares the child to become an adult.

The Mother Within

This is the same–but flipped–as the 'the father within' description, where not many have a radiant feminine mother. Many mothers are masculinized into a survival state and struggle to bestow truly feminine traits like vulnerability and shameless expression to their children. Add on top of that the toxins in society that obstruct their livers, pituitary, hypothalamus, pineal, and beyond to disrupt hormonal balance.

The mother helps the adult to remember that they can still be as fun and free-spirited as a child.

Feminine Presenting

When this term is used in the world of polarity, it is used to describe women who seem feminine in their looks, their way of speaking, and their walk. Many people today genuinely believe this is what femininity is. Feminine presentation often comes with an underlying ego that tends to come with a judgmental attitude held internally.

This kind of woman isn't the majority of the time thinking positively of others, and may struggle with true vulnerability and receptivity.

The *Warrioress* archetype is the most likely to be like this, whereas the *babygirl* archetype is already often naturally feminine in her presentation.

Masculine Presenting

Masculine presenting, in terms of polarity, refers to men acting with typical masculine bravado like they're faking it until they make it, but they lack the core constitution of masculinity. They may be lacking various masculine traits, such as the ability to confront harsh realities, the courage to stand up against tyrannical authority, and the choice of stoicism over drama, among others.

This man is often prone to being deceptive at least somewhere in his life because he is often a *Manifestor* archetype with the ability to use the female side of his mind to twist the truth.

The Developmental Archetypes have their own section under Proposed Hypothesis and Perspective - Psychology.

Top-down

This term represents a methodology or pattern that is utilized to achieve a result from a mental and or spiritual focus.

An example can be that a psychologist would take a top-down approach by utilizing psychological scientific principles to support their mental well-being.

Bottom-up

This term represents a methodology or pattern that is utilized to achieve a result from a bodily and foundational standpoint.

An example can be that a nutritionist may suggest a change of diet for their client, and that diet change can, on a physical level, positively impact their mental health.

Mission

The mission symbolizes a masculine path to accomplishing a goal. It is essentially the 'how' in achieving **the** 'purpose.'

Purpose

The purpose is a feminine aspect regarding the pursuit of a higher meaning, a path that transcends the flesh and is more spiritual in nature. One example of this is how my mom, early on, oriented my sister and I toward positively impacting the world. Her mention of the sex slave trade struck a chord with me, and for much of my life, I have been searching for ways to stop it. This book is one of those efforts, as I believe that healing society will significantly reduce the demand.

Cheerleader

Cheerleader energy is exactly as it sounds and is a core element of a woman's ability to inspire a man to greatness. She's not just a cheerleader for the man she loves but for those around her too. With her partner, she doesn't shoulder the heavy lifting to get him moving. Instead, through her powerful vulnerability, she activates his primal urge to protect something so soft and beautiful. He can't afford to collapse when her safety is on the line. With her beside him, he'll achieve far more than he ever could alone. That's cheerleader energy.

Analogies

This section is devoted to the analogies I frequently use to describe polarity.

The cactus analogy is probably the most popular, where a woman who is battered by life—primarily adult boys who take from her—develops a spiky fortress around her for future men to climb and disarm, all while she has a nice flower on top of the cactus.

This analogy symbolizes a traumatized woman.

What I teach is for women to see that this is a naïve response to being hurt because what happens is that she ends up attracting even more boys by developing defensive and masculine mechanisms when encountering men. Men who don't have fathers, or have father wounds in some areas, can tend to perpetuate boyhood well into their adult lives and will take this to their romantic relationships.

Her goal is to return to her essence as a flower, exploring the strength that emerges from embracing vulnerability. Its stem and petals are still very much capable of survival, but what separates the flower from the cactus is that the flower can draw in fierce protectors to ensure its survival from being stepped on and brutalized. This was supposed to happen for these girls who became a cactus, but they either disregarded male protection or didn't have it. This often stems from the fractures within our society and relationship dynamics today.

The ship analogy is something I use to describe what a man offers a woman. He ports at the dock at a local town, has his own crew, supplies, and mission he is oriented toward, but lacks purpose because he has no women on board; the crew is bedraggled from a hard journey to port, and so the softness offered by a muse becomes a high priority. However, the leader of this ship is selective; he will not take just any muse. He wants a woman who is capable enough to handle the conditions but focused on her role, where the men there have the masculine side of the job handled.

She is given the choice to set sail with him, knowing she would be giving him control, and that the ship won't be stopping for some time. This is a process where the woman fully lets go and gives him command to lead so she can focus on expression.

While the ship could wreck under his leadership, and the muse has valid reasons to critique him, a truly great muse understands that a remarkable man is often his own harshest critic. In this context, her role as a supportive cheerleader becomes essential, as she demonstrates her unwavering belief in him, ultimately benefiting the situation. She should be cheering him on well through the turbulence of the shipwreck all the way to a nearby island. Even on that desolate island, enduring hunger, she should strive to maintain a positive outlook and uplift the energy around her. After all, he might just find a way to gather palm trees and coconuts, crafting a means to escape their predicament. When they make it home, they have now grown even closer together and fully trust one another to get through anything.

There is, of course, the chance that they all drown and die, but that's the risk you take while living with a man who is a risk-taker and marker-pusher in life. They provide a wild ride, but not all of them make it to the top.

The jar-opener analogy is to encourage women to truly appreciate those small moments when a man opens a jar for them, reflecting on the feelings that arise in such instances. This process fosters gratitude and humility, creating a powerful dynamic where he feels fulfilled in being able to assist her, while she embraces the strength of calling upon a capable man for help, albeit a small task.

Quick Scientific Insights

In this section, I've captured some insightful scientific realities we have about relationship polarity, albeit few.

Keep in mind that I hold the belief that 95% of the studies that exist are flawed and potentially incorrect. Studies are valuable for providing insights into various issues, but they seldom deliver absolute truths. Instead, they should serve to reinforce arguments by combining empirical findings with anecdotal evidence and common sense, as their role is primarily to support rather than definitively conclude.

Anthropological Tribes

Some anthropological studies indicate that in certain tribal cultures, men may experience an increase in testosterone levels when they perceive themselves as *providers* of a substantial food bounty. This perception can lead to heightened status and *respect* within their community.

> *"Despite circadian declines in hormone levels, testosterone and cortisol of Tsimane hunters increased at the time of a kill and remained high as successful hunters returned home. However, if signaling male quality by 'showing off' was a larger relative driver of men's hunting behavior, one would expect greater hormonal response in cases where men returned with large sharable kills, especially in the presence of community members."*

Reference: PMC3871326

Boys Gain Testosterone Performing in Front of Women

One fascinating study is the "Skateboarder Study," where young men at a skatepark completed stunts in front of beautiful women. An increase in testosterone was observed in conjunction with the guys performing for the women, rather than for the other guys.

Women See Rises in Testosterone While in a Position of Power

There are also studies where women, when perceiving power, show elevated levels of testosterone.

"We found that wielding power increased testosterone in women compared with a control, regardless of whether it was performed in gender-stereotyped masculine or feminine ways."

Reference: 112 (45) 13805-13810

Men's testosterone drops when the baby is born

There are studies on men experiencing a drop in testosterone when they perceive their baby is about to be born. This is likely due to the need to access more of the feminine side of their mind, becoming more empathetic and present during the birth to provide the love and care required for the child.

Reference: 108 (39) 16194-16199

Child Bonding Hormones Between Dad & Mom

Research suggests that bonding hormones play a significant role in the relationship between children and their parents, but the nature of bonding differs between mothers and fathers. In general, oxytocin, a hormone linked to social bonding, is released during affectionate interactions with both parents. However, the triggers vary.

- For mothers, oxytocin is more likely activated through nurturing behaviors such as snuggling and caregiving.

- For fathers, bonding often comes through physical play, like roughhousing or active games, which stimulates oxytocin release. This unique form of play strengthens emotional bonds, contributing to emotional development and a child's sense of security.

Studies have observed that fathers who engage in more physical play with their children create stronger emotional connections through these shared activities.

Concluding Quick Scientific Insights

While we have access to many scientific publications that infer the realities of the sexes, this field is still fairly infantile and needs much further exploration.

Polarity in Modern Society

Movements Pushing Polarity

The term *polarity* has been trending a lot lately in the dating and relationship spheres online, symbolizing something similar to the dynamics often played out in a *traditional marriage*. The term *tradwife* has been thrown around frequently, with women on social media showcasing their lives as homemakers focused on being supportive wives. The intent of this book is to bring clarity to the term *polarity* and elevate it beyond the limited perception of being merely a trend or a cult.

Separately, many influencers and coaches have taken up the charge of defining the term and laying out structures and systems for people to understand how it works.

I'm here to tell the reader that while much of what they teach can be correct, some of their teachings have errors—often due to pure projection or passed-down knowledge such as culture, personal coaches, and religious influences. The reason I feel confident that what I am detailing here is more accurate is that these influencers generally learned from a top-down approach on how to be masculine or feminine, rather than experiencing what it's like to be both, and to heal from the imbalance. Further, I stay focused on keeping a sharp blade metered by research and debate alike. I always allow people to challenge my beliefs, in which case, if their logic is stronger, I concede.

There are *polarity coaches* online who are very popular and run large private groups for people to join, with various tiering systems based on what the client pays. One of the largest groups on Facebook has a multi-tiered educational program involving coaching. These groups are tightly regulated, where women and men alike are shadow-banned for speaking out in ways that go against the structure set by their leaders and expectations of their members.

While I believe much of what they teach is valuable, a lot is exaggerated or mixed with logical fallacies, which I will explain throughout this book.

Another side of polarity in society comes from a crowd that believes hyper-masculinity is the answer—where men are taught not to show emotion, vulnerability, or empathy, out of fear that women will lose attraction to them. I have addressed this argument in the *Common Objections* section of the book.

Where did polarity go and why is it coming back?

Over the past 30 to 50 years, the idea of men leading in relationships has steadily diminished. Women earned the right to vote in the 1920s, and by 1971, the formation of the National Women's Political Caucus marked a shift as women began to take on significant political power in the United States.

By the late 1990s, generally starting in the 1960s, some women were able to achieve six-figure salaries, and from there, female empowerment appeared boundless. Today, we see men becoming increasingly comfortable splitting the bill on dates, while women often lead in relationships, handle finances, and take on commanding roles in household dynamics. My own past experience of submission to women reflects a relationship trend that has gained traction.

Having transitioned to a different perspective on these dynamics and assisted women in moving away from such arrangements towards more balanced and polarized partnerships, I now recognize the flaws in the previous system with greater clarity.

Marriage rates are at an all-time low. According to the American Psychological Association, roughly 40–50% of first marriages end in divorce. As I write this, countless posts circulate online, asking, "What's going wrong with relationships?" and "Why aren't they working?"

The root societal issue—aside from health—is that we've created an environment where women struggle to trust men. This mistrust stems from two main sources: men who abused their power in the past and men today who fail to attain power due to inadequate competence, often compounded by low testosterone. While many women may long to relinquish control and trust capable men, doing so is increasingly difficult when the men around them lack capacity or drive.

Men aren't solely to blame, though. Women hold a vital, often unacknowledged role as muses. When a woman inspires a man, she adds vibrancy to his otherwise black-and-white grind. However, this dynamic reverses when women take on masculine roles—criticizing, commanding, or punishing men. Such patterns make it hard for men to reclaim leadership, even with the right intentions and healthier mentalities.

Economically and relationally, as women increasingly assume traditionally masculine roles, men are finding their role less valued, which in turn can diminish their drive and testosterone levels. Already, the average male testosterone level in the U.S. is alarmingly low at around 300 ng/dL. Without intervention, these averages could continue to decline, leading to a future where men lack the capacity to address wrongs or take risks—qualities positively correlated with higher testosterone levels.

Men need to feel needed to align with their purpose. Without this, they slip into comfort and complacency. On the other hand, women may not realize how much they lose by taking control, forfeiting their potential to be muses—not only to men but also to the world around them. While women's rights are non-negotiable, there's a balance to be struck. A return to allowing capable, kind, masculine men to lead can unlock greater fulfillment for both sexes.

Polarity in the Past

Historically, most human systems we know of were structured as patriarchies. There are arguments that some societies functioned matriarchally, particularly in indigenous tribes where women were occasionally elevated as leaders. What stands out in those cases is that this elevation often stemmed from their heightened feminine intuition—a gift that allowed them to lead not just with authority but with a deeply connected sense of foresight.

Yet when women are placed in roles that demand masculine traits—direct confrontation, heightened logic, or the necessity to maintain an inflated ego—something shifts. These actions are not inherently wrong or unnatural, but they come at a cost to the physiology and energy that enhance feminine intuition. Based on the science that exists, I believe sex hormones don't operate entirely in unison; they often oscillate. You can't hold both peak masculine and feminine qualities simultaneously—they trade places, always in flux. This oscillation matters. It speaks to why embracing one state fully often requires a softening or a letting go of the other.

Women who step into leadership to survive or adapt often develop extraordinary resilience, but I've seen how this resilience can erode something else—something equally vital. In my work with women who've taken on these roles, their intuitive strengths often seem dulled compared to those who prioritize softness, surrender, and vulnerability. It's not that the intuition disappears. It's more like it whispers rather than sings.

This isn't about limiting women to roles of passivity. It's about observing what's gained—and what's quietly lost—when women feel they must lead through masculine modes rather than aligning with their natural feminine rhythm.

Survival

In the health world, I often teach from the perspective that humans began as hunters and gatherers within tribal communities, surviving together in an ecosystem that required harmony with nature. This framework is vital because the bulk of scientific research into optimal health supports the idea that living in the wild—or at least emulating its principles—is the foundation of well-being.

There's an alternative belief rooted in certain religious systems, particularly Biblical ones, that humans were created fully equipped to cultivate crops, herd livestock, and control fire. While I believe in God, I don't subscribe to this view. The evidence overwhelmingly shows that ancient humans depended primarily on hunting and foraging, and this reliance on nature shaped who we are today.

When I was five, I had an innate ability to catch snakes and lizards by the handful. Today, I'd be lucky to grab one without a trap. There's something primal in boys that seems wired for hunting from an early age. Even as I write this, I saw a young boy near to where I live who mastered catching lizards. One has even bonded with him, riding his back as he walks around. Boys, from the beginning, are equipped to contribute to their tribe as hunters.

Girls, however, develop differently. Their early instincts lean toward connection. Studies show that at just 12 months, girls separated from their mothers by a barrier are likely to cry, while by 24 months, they are more likely than boys to ask for help in overcoming the obstacle.

> *"At 12 months, girls were likely to cry when placed behind a barrier separating them from their mothers, but by 24 months, they were more likely than boys to ask for help to overcome the barrier."*

– PMC3293480

This doesn't make girls weaker—it makes them uniquely skilled in leveraging indirect paths to achieve their goals. Women's ability to gather support is an extraordinary competency that often goes untapped or misused in modern society. Imagine the potential if this ability were honed: a person sharing their struggles with a billionaire in a persuasive way, could possibly receive $50,000 to rebuild her life. This level of persuasive power, when mastered, is transformative. *This is in no way suggests using deceit or manipulation, rather, it illustrates the beauty of a woman in her feminine and vulnerable element.*

In contrast, men, while similarly capable of persuasion, are less likely to approach vulnerability in the same way. This disparity means women often receive more assistance through emotional appeals. It's not a matter of fairness, but of human nature—a reflection of deeply ingrained tribal dynamics.

Returning to a tribal way of living, or at least incorporating its elements, is critical for realigning with our natural blueprint. Comparing the tribal lifestyle to the modern first-world existence reveals how far we've drifted from the principles that kept us healthy and harmonious. As society marches forward, the illusion of progress seems to correlate with declining physical and emotional well-being.

In tribal settings, life was polarized. Men, wired for adversity and growth, took the physical risks of the hunt. Women, while capable of hunting, were more effective in roles centered around nurturing, connection, and gathering. This division wasn't about limiting anyone but about optimizing survival. Unlike lions, where females often lead the hunt, human women are biologically less suited for such tasks. No amount of hormonal intervention, trauma, or ego-boosting can override the physical and psychological differences between masculine men and feminine women.

Don't get me wrong, women **can** hunt, just as men **can** be nurturing, but the pursuit of survival is best accomplished when men hunt and women direct their focus toward people within the tribe.

The natural order remains undeniable. Masculine men thrive on challenge and physical risk, while feminine women often find their power in connection, intuition, and resourcefulness. Of course, exceptions exist—certain archetypes or conditions like PCOS may influence a woman's propensity for hunting or risk-taking. But these are deviations, not the norm. Understanding these dynamics is not about imposing limits; it's about honoring the inherent strengths that make us human.

Survival Conclusion

Survival in many tribal societies was a balance of complementary roles. Men and women were not merely fulfilling assigned duties; their roles were shaped by their natural abilities, optimizing survival. Men hunted and protected, while women nurtured relationships and gathered resources. Today, this balance is disrupted in modern society, which tends to prioritize individual achievement over communal strength. This disconnect from our tribal roots is linked to many health and societal issues, as we no longer function within a cooperative, survival-oriented environment. Reclaiming some elements of this structure could support better health, resilience, and community living.

Ladies & Gentlemen

Serve the lady first: open the door for her, guide her across the puddle, take her hand, and lead her. Less than a century ago, the streets were filled with ladies and gentlemen, yet, in a remarkably short span, we have largely seen their disappearance. There are many arguments regarding what happened, with some believing it's simply "the times" and that we must adapt to an ever-changing world. However, under the *Polarity Basics: Health* section of this book, I discuss the health problems we've faced over the last century. Additionally, in "Where did polarity go and why is it coming back?" I explore the societal issues that have contributed to this shift.

Gentlemen of the past largely cherished women, and women felt both respected and safe because of this. To be cherished meant being held in high regard as a lady who was delicate, yet strong. Men would build skyscrapers inspired by these women, and with gentlemen handling the physical world and bringing home provision, women could fully express themselves as wives and mothers.

Certainly, history includes many negatives, and no polarized relationship from that time was likely perfect. However, these historical examples are some of the most recent we have to better understand "traditional relationships" and their connection to polarity.

Polarity in the Past Conclusion

Regardless of what the past has shown us, it is raw instinct, intuition, and hormonal health that serve as the compass to the blueprint, and nothing else can ever show enough merit to supersede this principle. Our bodies are the way home – the path to the truth.

Proposed Hypothesis and Perspective - Psychology

The Polarities

This has been my hypothesis over the years: there are two sides of the mind, the feminine and the masculine, which could be referred to as yin and yang - the polarities. In gathering data for this book, I learned that Carl Jung proposed something similar, referring to the 'Anima' and the 'Animus.' Jung described the animus as the unconscious masculine side of a woman, and the anima as the unconscious feminine side of a man.

Everything we do throughout the day can carry masculine or feminine energy, often mixed in various ratios, much like how communication takes place. For example, punching someone in the chest is macroscopically masculine, but the reason *why* someone would do that could often be feminine, and where the punch lands can lean either way.

I don't want to overcomplicate this, so let's break it down...

If you had Leonidas of the 300 Spartans in front of you, how would you rate his level of masculinity on a scale from 1 to 100? Based on historical evidence, I'd estimate he maintained an 85 out of 100, where 100 is impossible to achieve and wouldn't be ideal. Some of his men might be in the 90s, even though Leonidas is clearly the leader. Why? Because he was good at speaking to his men and leading them, which means he had more empathy than a brute. This empathy would come at the expense of his raw masculinity. Yes, great leadership requires empathy. A man without empathy may be respected, but he's not going to be truly great. He might be feared and competent, but not loved by his people.

Now, how do we begin to understand the masculinity within a woman or the femininity within a man?

Masculinity in Women

Women need masculinity within them to live at all.

Imagine a hunter-gatherer woman back at camp while the man is out hunting. If a predator enters the camp and attempts to take one of the children, is it realistic to think she would be completely helpless? No. Women do need to tap into masculinity intermittently, especially in moments of survival. Let me emphasize this: **women must sometimes embody the masculine traits of strength and ferocity when the situation demands it**. Sadly, in today's world, many women keep the masculine aspect of themselves at the forefront, as part of their identity—almost like shield-maidens fighting in a never-ending war.

If men were able—and willing—to perform their roles, no healthy feminine woman would want to take on a masculine role in their own lives.

The masculinization of women today stems from many factors. Historically, there have been many women with masculine traits, but I believe these women are that way due to an imbalance in their lives. Whether it's because they had a father who wanted a son, were thrust into survival situations, were overly influenced by external forces seeking power, had heavy metal toxicity, ate too much grain leading to biounavailable copper buildup, or were exposed to mercury in the womb—these imbalances all disrupt the natural blueprint we were designed for.

Femininity in Men

I often hear that there's an agenda created by society to convince us that men have femininity within them, subtly emasculating men. While it's true that societal forces can mislead both men and women in various ways, it is also true that men do have femininity within them.

In the Hormones section of the Proposed Hypothesis and Perspective - Physiology chapter, I explain the basics of male and female hormones in the human system. Men, for instance, often exhibit femininity when they take on nurturing roles, such as when a child is born. This is usually accompanied by an elevation in estrogen, which biologically confirms the presence of femininity in men.

As mentioned earlier, Leonidas could not have been the leader he was without tapping into the feminine side of his mind. This feminine energy gave him the communication skills necessary to lead and be heard by his people. **A man's speech would be incomplete without this feminine aspect contributing to his communication.**

Additionally, men may need to access their nurturing side if something were to happen to the mother and there's no one else around to fill that role. Ideally, if we were living in alignment with the natural blueprint, the tribe would step in to help, allowing men and women to stay true to their roles.

Core Psychology

From a psychological perspective, one can categorize the feminine and masculine sides of the mind under the terms 'agency' and 'receptivity.'

Agency refers to an individual's capacity to act independently, make choices, and exert control over their own life and environment. It involves self-directed actions that demonstrate autonomy, intentionality, and the ability to influence outcomes. In psychology, agency is often linked to concepts like personal empowerment, self-efficacy, and the belief that one's actions can change or shape the course of events.

Receptivity refers to an individual's capacity to be open and responsive to external influences, whether those are emotions, experiences, or interactions with others. It involves allowing, receiving, and processing external stimuli with a degree of openness and adaptability, rather than taking action or trying to exert control. Receptivity is often associated with emotional attunement, vulnerability, and the ability to go with the flow of life's circumstances.

In a polarity sense, agency would be referred to as 'giving,' or 'doing.' Receptivity would be seen as 'receiving,' or 'being.'

Under agency, we have competency, and under receptivity, we have vulnerability.

Competency is mastery, self-reliance, and an ability to handle challenges independently. It's about possessing the skills, knowledge, and confidence to manage situations without needing external assistance, which is traditionally seen as a more "masculine" trait.

Vulnerability involves an openness to experiencing situations without complete control or guaranteed safety. It's the willingness to rely on others, accept potential limitations, and openly feel and show emotions. This is often seen as a more "feminine" trait because it emphasizes connection, trust, and receptivity.

From there, it goes on and on...

Objectivity vs. Subjectivity

Instinct vs. Intuition

Independence vs. Collaboration

Discipline vs. Flexibility

Confrontation vs. Appeasement

Stoicism vs. Expression

Giving vs. Receiving

Respect vs. Love

Mission vs. Purpose

You get the picture.

Both sexes utilize both sides of their minds to varying degrees, as explained earlier. Without these psychological constructs, there would be no humanity, and no masculinity or femininity.

ADD/ADHD & ASD

[Hybrids that combine traits of both ASD (autism spectrum disorder) and ADHD (attention deficit hyperactive disorder) are not covered in this book, but will be explored in more depth through other projects.]

If there's anything that can make relationships or hormonal health particularly challenging, it's the interplay between the Attention Deficit Hyperactive Disorder (ADD/ADHD) and Autism Spectrum Disorder (ASD) tendencies, reflecting a split between the masculine and feminine sides of the brain. While it's not inherently wrong to engage in relationships while experiencing this split, it's critically important to understand the potential pitfalls. These are dynamics I've spent years examining and refining through my own experiences.

In the broader context, we observe individuals who are distinctly ASD or ADD/ADHD, alongside others with milder symptoms who may not even consider themselves neurodivergent. Personally, I identify more with ADD (not ADHD), leaning heavily into common tendencies for the disorder in the past. I used to have such a broad understanding of life that 'deductive reasoning' felt maddening. Over time, I've developed a greater appreciation for balance, integrating more of the opposite side of my mind.

Now let's delve into the cognitive split between the masculine and feminine aspects of the brain. ASD appears to align with a more imbalanced masculine form of neurodivergence, while ADD/ADHD reflects a more imbalanced feminine cognitive framework. Below, you'll find a synthesized explanation of these two tendencies and their connection to the masculine-feminine divide. My understanding has been shaped through years of immersion among individuals strongly expressing either ADD/ADHD or ASD traits.

ASD Basic traits:

- Inability to maintain eye contact
- Trouble assessing social cues
- Anxiety in social settings
- Difficulty with verbal communication nuances (jokes, sarcasm)
- Rituals and restrictive habits
- Easily overwhelmed by sensory input
- Adherence to strict routines
- Notices sensory input others don't
- Difficulty in two-way conversations
- Ability to hyper-focus on specific interests
- Experiences emotions intensely
- Frustration with small changes or disruptions
- Sensitivity to light, noise, or smell
- Difficulty with transitions; often late
- Prefers listening and observing over speaking and interacting
- Often seen as rude or blunt
- Perfectionism in certain areas
- Prefers working at home or alone
- Avoids stressful social situations
- May be perceived as selfish
- Difficulty tracking multiple conversations
- Tends to take things literally

ADD Basic traits:

- Careless mistakes and lack of detail

- Difficulty sustaining attention

- Impulsivity

- Divergent thinking

- Seems not to listen when spoken to

- Does not follow through on instructions

- Difficulty organizing tasks and activities

- Avoids tasks requiring sustained mental effort

- Loses things needed for tasks

- Easily distracted

- Forgetful in daily activities

Feminine-leaning traits:

1. Spontaneity / Impulsiveness

- **Feminine Aspect**: Quick to adapt or respond to new stimuli, embracing change easily. This can manifest as an openness to new experiences, ideas, and environments. Rather than sticking rigidly to a plan, the feminine energy flows where attention goes.

- **Masculine Contrast**: Structured decision-making, deliberate actions based on predefined goals or principles.

2. Creativity / Divergent Thinking

- **Feminine Aspect**: The ability to think outside the box, allowing for broader, non-linear connections between ideas. This expansive thinking is often associated with emotional or intuitive leaps rather than logical progression.

- **Masculine Contrast**: Linear, goal-oriented thinking with a focus on efficiency and staying within boundaries.

3. Emotional Variability / Sensitivity

- **Feminine Aspect**: Shifting emotional states and a heightened sensitivity to the surrounding environment. This broad emotional range allows for adaptability and empathetic connection to others but may feel inconsistent to outside observers.

- **Masculine Contrast**: Emotional steadiness or neutrality, often seen as a consistent emotional baseline or "rock."

4. Distractibility / Flexibility

- **Feminine Aspect**: Attention that flows from one focus to another, allowing for multi-tasking or the ability to manage multiple domains simultaneously. This flexibility can be seen as being "in the moment" and responding to a wide range of stimuli.

- **Masculine Contrast**: Singular focus and staying on task, providing structure and consistency over time.

5. Curiosity / Exploration

- **Feminine Aspect**: Constantly seeking new experiences and information, this openness to discovery can appear as inconsistency but is a reflection of a broader, exploratory nature. Curiosity is expansive and non-linear.

- **Masculine Contrast**: Grounded in mastery and depth in a few areas, rather than exploring a broad range of interests.

6. Fluidity in Time Management

- **Feminine Aspect**: A more intuitive relationship with time, where schedules and tasks are approached with flexibility. There's a natural flow rather than rigid adherence to deadlines.

- **Masculine Contrast**: Structured time management, punctuality, and consistent scheduling, providing clear boundaries and stability.

7. Connection-Oriented Communication

- **Feminine Aspect**: ADHD individuals often exhibit communication styles that are open-ended, circular, or tangential. This can create broad, engaging conversations that don't necessarily stick to a specific point but allow for relational depth and connection.

- **Masculine Contrast**: Focused, direct communication aimed at achieving a specific outcome or goal.

8. Restlessness / Need for Change

- **Feminine Aspect**: A desire for constant movement, change, and novelty can reflect a feminine archetype of cyclical patterns and the rejection of static states. This restlessness fuels adaptability.

- **Masculine Contrast**: Stability and contentment in repetition, grounded in predictability and routine.

9. Embracing Chaos / Nonlinear Thinking

- **Feminine Aspect**: An openness to chaos, where not everything has to be neatly ordered or structured. The ability to function in ambiguity or thrive in environments where things are in flux.

- **Masculine Contrast**: Preference for order, structure, and clarity.

10. Seeking Variety in Tasks and Experiences

- **Feminine Aspect**: Enjoying a wide range of interests or activities at once, moving from one task to another based on intuition or emotion. This variety-seeking behavior reflects a more fluid, adaptable energy that's not confined to one path.

- **Masculine Contrast**: Staying with one task until it's completed, prioritizing focus and discipline over the need for variety.

Masculine-leaning traits:

1. Rigid Thinking / Focus on Rules

- ☯ **Masculine Aspect**: A strong adherence to rules, patterns, and logical frameworks. This creates structure and predictability, which are often comforting and stabilizing for those with ASD.

- ☯ **Feminine Contrast**: More flexible and adaptable thinking, open to bending rules or making exceptions based on emotions or context.

2. Singular Focus / Deep Special Interests

- ☯ **Masculine Aspect**: The ability to focus intensely on a single topic or activity for extended periods, developing a deep mastery or understanding. This focus on depth over breadth reflects a grounded, linear approach.

- ☯ **Feminine Contrast**: Broader, more exploratory interests that jump from one subject to another, with less emphasis on mastery and more on variety.

3. Preference for Routine and Consistency

- ☯ **Masculine Aspect**: A strong preference for structure, routine, and predictability in daily life. This creates a solid foundation where safety and comfort come from knowing what to expect.

- ☯ **Feminine Contrast**: Flexibility and spontaneity, where change and unpredictability are welcomed as opportunities for growth.

4. Literal Thinking / Logical Reasoning

- **Masculine Aspect**: A literal, logical approach to understanding the world. Things are seen as they are, with a focus on clear definitions and factual accuracy, which mirrors a masculine energy of grounded reasoning.

- **Feminine Contrast**: More abstract or intuitive thinking, where emotions, symbols, or metaphor may play a larger role in interpretation.

5. Emotional Regulation / Detachment

- **Masculine Aspect**: Often, people with ASD may struggle with expressing emotions outwardly, presenting a more emotionally neutral or detached demeanor. This can align with the masculine trait of emotional steadiness or rationality.

- **Feminine Contrast**: Emotional variability, sensitivity, and expression, where emotions are felt and displayed more openly or fluidly.

6. Direct, Concise Communication

- **Masculine Aspect**: Communication is often straightforward and to the point, without much use of metaphor, emotional undertones, or indirect cues. This aligns with a masculine approach to communication, focusing on clarity and efficiency.

- **Feminine Contrast**: Indirect, relational communication that might rely on emotional nuance, tone, or subtext to convey meaning.

7. Problem-Solving through Logic and Patterns

- **Masculine Aspect**: The ability to solve problems through logical analysis and recognizing patterns, often working through challenges in a methodical, step-by-step manner. This reflects a masculine focus on structure and solutions.

- **Feminine Contrast**: Intuitive problem-solving, where emotions, connections, and flexibility guide the process rather than strict logic.

8. Detail-Oriented / Precision in Interests

- **Masculine Aspect**: A strong focus on detail, exactness, and precision. Those with ASD often excel in areas requiring close attention to detail and adherence to exact standards, which reflects a masculine focus on accuracy and consistency.

- **Feminine Contrast**: Broad thinking and creativity, where the bigger picture is often more important than the finer details.

9. Structured Social Interactions

- **Masculine Aspect**: Social interactions for those with ASD are often structured around clear, logical frameworks, such as knowing the "rules" of conversation or what's appropriate in certain social contexts. This provides a solid framework for navigating complex social environments.

- **Feminine Contrast**: Social interactions that are more fluid, intuitive, and based on reading emotional or relational cues, which may change depending on context.

10. Strong Need for Control

- **Masculine Aspect**: A need for control over one's environment or schedule, where predictability and certainty provide a sense of security. This can show up in managing sensory input, organizing surroundings, or setting clear boundaries.

- **Feminine Contrast**: Adaptability to changing environments, being open to going with the flow and responding to the moment.

Disruptions in neurological function can significantly affect femininity or masculinity within a relationship. For example, someone leaning heavily into ASD may become too rigid on certain issues or struggle to grasp broad, nuanced topics. On the other hand, someone with ADD may find highly systematized, linear topics overwhelming due to the level of detail condensed into a specific framework.

In a relationship dynamic where the man has ADD and the woman has ASD (a personal one for me), the ASD woman is likely to hold strong judgments about the man's lack of structure or organization. She would naturally gravitate toward a sense of routine, structure, and order, whereas the ADD man would approach life more broadly with spontaneity; often perceived as chaotic to women. Even if the ADD man explains something in great detail, the ASD woman might struggle to understand it because his explanation lacks the linearity and predictability she prefers.

Understanding these dynamics is crucial to avoid common pitfalls in relationships. And this is just scratching the surface. When you factor in systems like the Enneagram, Jung's Archetypes, Myers-Briggs (MBTI), astrology, or even the Developmental Archetypes mentioned in this book, the layers of complexity further deepen.

Conclusion of ADD/ADHD & ASD

One big lesson to take away, which is at the root of this split cognitively, is that while some people have both forms of this neurodivergence, one or the other, or none at all, it often leads to **misunderstandings** that are often to blame for much of relationship failures across the board. It is crucial to be able to understand your lover if you plan to be together for multiple years or more.

Astrology

Astrology is a dense topic with much speculation, so this section of the book only serves as acknowledgment of it adding nuance to the ever-expanding study of understanding human psychology.

I personally account for astrology in my personal life. For example, my sister once thought I was autistic because I often cut through social norms to directly state the truth. This could be seen as something someone with ASD might do, as they tend to struggle with social gray areas and can be overly direct. However, what I actually had was really bad ADD, where I lose track of what I'm going to say and end up blurting it out before losing the thought entirely through impulse—sometime in the past I'd even drift off into "dreamland," miles away from the conversation.

On top of that, I focus on and cut straight to the truth for two reasons: one, because I love stirring the pot, and two, because I'm a Gemini who thrives on debate and getting down to the raw truth. With all of that combined, I'll absolutely cut right through social norms to lay it out plainly for people, therefore it may appear that my ADD is as bad as ever. In my view, astrology absolutely plays a role here.

Astrology also blends with the Developmental Archetypes. For instance, Gemini *babygirls* and Leo *babygirls* can have inherent traits, like poor judgment in discerning a lover, but they can differ in other areas. The Gemini *babygirl* might be more prone to being deceitfully sweet, while the Leo *babygirl* might lean towards being argumentative or combative, often driven by self-righteousness.

Dominance & Submission

In relationships, dominance and submission often reflect traditional gender roles—men as protectors and leaders, women as nurturers and supporters. While these dynamics can be natural, especially in evolutionary contexts, they are often misunderstood when applied to alternative sexual roles, where dominance and submission can take on psychological or fetishistic meanings. Thus, while rooted in nature, the interpretation of these terms can vary widely depending on context.

Dominance

In nature, dominance is an intrinsic force that compels those who cannot oppose it to submit. However, when dominance is wielded without the willing submission of others, it can lead to manipulation and harm. This imbalance often results in a negative perception of dominance, as many who hold power may use it in ways that harm those around them. The ability to dominate is pervasive, and few can manage it without corruption creeping in.

Nonetheless, dominance is essential for survival. Throughout history, humans have operated within hierarchical structures. The man with the most merit often rises to a position of power, gaining influence over others. This type of man often becomes a leader, guiding the decisions of a group or tribe through a kind of meritocracy. People willingly submit to his leadership, recognizing his ability to wield power effectively.

In romantic relationships, the natural order often grants dominance to the man, aligning with traditional roles. As the dominant figure, he leads in taking on the real-world challenges, while the woman, in her own sphere of influence, love and connection, inspiring those around her. While modern dynamics sometimes see women taking dominant roles, they do so through their own inner masculinity, as masculinity is often synonymous with dominance.

Submission

The concept of 'submission' in relationships is often viewed negatively today, but it's important to recognize that both dominance and submission are fundamental to life.

When a woman submits to a man, it opens doors for both individuals. A man who is motivated by the protective instinct inspired by a woman's vulnerability becomes more attuned to his role and grows stronger in his masculinity. Submission, in this sense, helps both partners step into more defined and empowered roles.

Looking at submission from a natural perspective offers clarity. For example, in the animal kingdom, submission isn't a weakness. The male honeybee submits his life to the queen, and even the queen submits her reproductive tract to the drone during mating. Submission is not exclusive to human relationships or polarized dynamics, and it plays a role in many species' survival.

In human relationships, submission can be seen as a gateway to creation. When a woman submits to a man, it allows for new life, the expansion of his purpose, and the inevitable uplifting of the community. It fosters a deep and profound connection, rooted in the balance between vulnerability and strength.

Radiant Femininity & Emanating Masculinity: The Ideal

Under the Loose Terms and Definitions section of the book, there are basic descriptions for emanating masculinity and radiant femininity.

A big problem we have today is that we lack examples of what the ideal woman and man look like, and this is likely due to the reasons stated earlier in the book, like societal beliefs, or our health as a whole.

Sure, everything in the world—especially with topics regarding humanity—is incredibly context-based, and so using the term 'ideal' may sound like an overstatement to the reader. However, merits are everything when it comes to the raw pursuit of survival that we are all bound to here on earth. My argument for radiant femininity and emanating masculinity is one supported by nature and merit.

What unites the radiant woman and the emanating man is their integration of bodily, mental, and spiritual health. Yet, as discussed in the Polarity Basics: Health section of the book, ideal levels for all three are unattainable in today's ailing world. As a result, our standards must be tempered. One might imagine Jesus or a Buddhist monk embodying spiritual health at its peak, a prehistoric caveman epitomizing physical health, and mental health being so closely tied to physical health as being difficult to define in historical terms.

Today, people might label someone as radiant or emanating based on their resemblance to these ideals. In history, few seem more masculine and merit-based than Leonidas of Sparta. His ability to subdue enemies threatening his home, combined with his openness to seek external support, reflects a profound balance of masculinity and femininity. While his spiritual health and every detail to his private life isn't fully known, his battle and leadership merits elevate him.

Identifying history's most radiant woman is challenging since women have often been confined to utilitarian roles that created imbalances, such as playing a masculine role part of the time. The greatest mothers likely never made headlines and were known only to a few. Personally, my mother is the most radiant woman among the many I've met. She balances femininity, marked by sweetness and softness, with discernment in situations requiring masculinity. I've witnessed her warmth and presence draw others in like a comforting fire, yet she actively seeks out the lost and alone to offer comfort. Femininity is a magnetic power of drawing people in; masculinity in a woman is the capacity to affect change in others. Radiance, therefore, emerges from a full integration of these polarities, and my mother exemplifies this balance better than anyone I know.

To keep it all very simple, the emanating masculine man and the radiant feminine woman are two people who have reached the *Balanced* archetype and have a higher touch where they think beyond their own needs to positively lift the world around them up.

Giving & Receiving

*"A man gives, a woman receives.
The adult gives, the child receives."*

This quote, often shared within the polarized relationship community, holds a profound truth that goes beyond its simplicity. Giving represents the masculine and adult role, while receiving embodies the feminine and childlike essence.

In a polarized relationship, a man primarily seeks to give, and a woman fulfills her role by receiving. Core aspects of what a man gives is provision, protection, stability, and direction, while she, in receiving these, offers nurturing, creativity, resonance, joyfulness, and more. When a man gives fully to a woman, it cultivates her ability to bring forth her best qualities.

This dynamic evolves when a man and woman reach a stage where they create and nurture life together. At this point, giving becomes a shared act, with both parents contributing pieces of themselves to their children. Children, being naturally in a state of receiving, depend on the giving capacity of fulfilled adults. However, when men and women are not personally fulfilled, they often give less than what their children need to thrive.

By integrating their opposite qualities—masculine/adult for the woman and feminine/child for the man—both partners reach a state of wholeness. This integration enables them to give completely, not only to each other but also to their children and the generations to come.

Yin & Yang in Polarity

The origins of Yin and Yang trace back to ancient Chinese philosophy, particularly in the *I Ching* (also known as the *Book of Changes*), which dates back to around the Western Zhou period (1046–771 BCE). This concept symbolizes duality, showing that seemingly opposing forces are actually interconnected, interdependent, and complementary rather than being complete opposites. Yin and Yang are not isolated; they are two parts of a whole, each containing the essence of the other. Yin represents qualities like femininity, passivity, receptivity, darkness, and the moon, while Yang embodies masculinity, activity, assertiveness, light, and the sun.

In the context of polarity, Yin and Yang correspond directly to the masculine and feminine forces. This dynamic interplay between the two is essential for balance and harmony. The concept of Yin-Yang extends beyond gender; it can apply to all aspects of life—light and dark, hot and cold, action and rest. When we apply polarity to relationships, the masculine aligns with the Yang principle (agency, assertiveness) and the feminine with the Yin principle (receptivity, emotional openness).

Achieving balance between these forces is crucial for both physical and emotional well-being. In relationships, the teachings of polarity reflect how men and women express different aspects of Yin and Yang, complementing each other's strengths. Just as Yin and Yang are meant to remain in balance without overpowering each other, so too should the masculine and feminine energies—when they complement each other, they create optimal harmony, both in life and in relationships.

Within each side of the Yin and Yang symbol is a seed that represents an aspect of each within one another. To clarify the earlier points about how femininity contains elements of masculinity and vice versa, this concept is essentially interconnected. The "dots" can be interpreted as the balance of femininity and masculinity that each person should possess. This is why I propose that an 85/15 ratio—favoring either femininity or masculinity—can be a reasonable guideline. In my experience, the most peak masculine men and feminine women tend to embody this balance. Unfortunately, in today's world and in my experience, most people do not reflect this 85/15 ratio due to the influences of our environment.

The goal is to work toward the balance that Yin & Yang visually present.

Concluding The Polarities

There is a great divide between the sexes today, and it's due to many different reasons—reasons so varied that it seems no one can reach a consensus. The Polarities section of the book is my humble attempt to bring more clarity from a natural viewpoint: that masculine men and feminine women are designed to operate harmoniously together, as if bound together like the two halves of Yin and Yang. We have unknowingly disrupted this blueprint, and I genuinely hope the reader continues on to learn more of what I have to share regarding polarity and my mission to unite the sexes.

Development: Orders of Fulfillment

The therapy industry is fueled by humanity's parental wounds, particularly from upbringing. Many think that poor upbringing is merely a product of societal breakdown or generational trauma, but the real root often lies in our physical health. Our ability to treat others with kindness or abuse is deeply connected to how our bodies and minds are functioning.

Throughout my career, I've had psychologists approach me to enhance their top-down models of mental health by incorporating bottom-up approaches I'd been studying. These methods are essential for reaching a higher state of health.

Growing up, I disconnected from my father, which left me lacking competency, even though my mother worked hard to give me a sense of agency. Still, there's only so much a mother can do without the father's role in a boy's life.

It wasn't until after years of cleansing and eating organically that I fully cleared much of the mental health struggles that had shaped my identity. By 28, I realized I had sought survival skills not just to live in the woods, but to become a man. My instincts led me to become competent, and I opened my heart to more masculine influences, which catalyzed my healing.

The path I followed wasn't just about food and cleansing—it was about **developing** both my psychological and physical **competency**. This shift in my development played a pivotal role in my transformation into a more masculine man, no longer leaning so strongly into the effeminate side of my character.

Over time, I've helped others help themselves through similar journeys, focusing on gut health and applying what I've learned about bottom-up and top-down approaches. This process led to the evolution of my business from Gut Goals LLC to Polarity Health LLC, focusing on optimizing endocrine and psychological health for individuals. It's about personal growth, inside and out.

The following section is critical. It connects my personal journey to the broader societal issues surrounding relationships and psychology today. I'm breaking down the fundamental roles that shape men's and women's lives, starting with childhood. Understanding these dynamics is essential for recognizing where things have gone wrong—and how we can begin to fix them.

Child Development

Childhood development lays the foundation for both psychological and hormonal health later in life. The presence of polarized parental roles—each contributing their unique strengths—is essential.

> *"Up to a quarter of all children globally live in single-parent households. Studies have concluded that children who grow up with continuously married parents have better health outcomes than children who grow up with single or separated parents."*

doi:10.1136/bmjopen-2020-043361

While this research focuses on the impact of divorce, it doesn't fully address the challenges that arise when single parents struggle with polarity. From what I've seen, single parents often lean too heavily into one role, leaving gaps in their children's development.

Boys (Ages 0-8)

In the early years, a boy's relationship with his mother is the cornerstone of his emotional and social development. A secure maternal bond teaches him how to express emotions, builds his confidence, and helps him form healthy social connections.

> *"Research backs this up—boys who had secure attachments to their mothers tend to grow up more emotionally secure and confident."*

doi.org/10.3389/fpsyg.2021.660866

By around age 8, the father's role becomes more central. This shift introduces the competencies and structures a boy needs to navigate the world as a man. Together, these influences shape his ability to connect emotionally and take on responsibilities.

Boys (Ages 8+)

As boys grow, the father's influence becomes vital. A strong bond with his dad helps him develop positive behaviors and a solid masculine identity. Between 8 and young adulthood, a father's guidance is crucial for preparing him to lead—whether in his family or his community.

> *"Father's love-related behaviors often have as strong or even stronger implications for children's psychological adjustment, personality, and socio-emotional development than do mother's love."*

DOI:10.4172/2471-271X.1000150

For me, this was a missing piece. By age 10, I had cut ties with my father, and that absence created struggles I had to work through later in life.

Girls (Ages 0-6)

From birth to age six, a girl's bond with her mother is fundamental. This relationship teaches her how to express emotions, build self-worth, and form meaningful social connections. A strong maternal connection fosters empathy, resilience, and confidence, laying the groundwork for healthy relationships in the future.

Girls (Ages 6+)

Around age six, the father's role becomes increasingly important. Positive interactions with her father during this stage build her sense of security, self-worth, and confidence. These lessons shape how she perceives herself and the world around her.

> *"Father presence in young girls, psychological security, achievement goal orientation, and resilience would be positively related."*
>
> *Result: Supported. Significant positive correlations were found between all variables.*

doi.org/10.3389/fpsyg.2024.1403403

A father's protection, guidance, and example of masculinity teach her about boundaries, resilience, and self-respect. These qualities prepare her for healthy, fulfilling relationships later in life.

Conclusion of Child Development

When children lack balanced contributions from both parents, imbalances often develop. If a mother wasn't nurturing or feminine, the father—or another figure—would need to compensate by bringing more of that energy into the child's life, and vice versa for masculinity.

There isn't much research specifically linking polarized parenting to hormone profiles, but my experiences with clients suggest these dynamics profoundly impact development. Children need these balanced examples to grow into their best selves.

This book exists because so many of these imbalances are now common. Addressing them isn't just about healing individuals—it's about reshaping our approach to parenting, relationships, and societal health.

Adult Fulfillment

I have not included a "young adult" section here because, in natural settings, boys historically reached manhood and girls blossomed into womanhood much earlier than they do today. It is reasonable to assume that many of their adult responsibilities and needs would have become relevant by around age 15, often marked by a 'rite of passage' certifying them as adults.

Men

When a boy develops a sense of **agency**, he gains the ability to fulfill his **mission(s)** and **purpose** through **competency**. This development sets the stage for him to create and sustain a family. To achieve this, he needs the resources, skills, and physical health that enhance his ability to attract and maintain a partnership. **A man's fulfillment often involves claiming a woman to build a family and imparting agency and competency to his children**. These traits are key to his role as a provider and protector.

Interestingly, dissociation from women can sometimes lead to alternative dynamics, such as the preference some gay male tops (the men who lean more dominant) have for younger men. In my observations, this preference may be rooted in their quest for agency or unresolved dynamics around masculinity.

When a man lacks fulfillment in areas like competency, it often manifests in his relationships. For example, a *Manifestor* archetype—who may lack a strong masculine example from a father figure—might unconsciously expect his lover to embody more masculine traits. Without competency, a man might struggle to attract women early in life, potentially leading to resentment toward women who rejected him during his weaker phases. Over time, this can alter his preferences in romantic partners or even diminish his interest in women altogether.

Men who perceive themselves as inadequate or incapable of leadership and provision often face profound shifts in their worldview and relationship dynamics. This struggle is most prevalent in the *Manifestor* archetype, as the *Balanced* and *Forger* archetypes typically excel in attracting relationships with women; maintaining them is a different story. These patterns reveal the critical role of competency in shaping a man's life and relationships.

The Developmental Archetypes section fully defines the archetypes mentioned in this section.

Women

When a woman develops vulnerability and receptivity, she aligns herself with her natural role of fostering emotional connection and nurturing relationships. Cultivating self-awareness, warmth, and care allows her to invite meaningful connections, particularly with a man who shares her values and vision for life. Her inner confidence and grace—often mirrored in her health and presence—naturally attracts others. When she commits to a man, she prepares herself to nurture and raise children, imparting empathy and receptivity to create a secure, supportive environment within which her children can thrive.

Because evolutionary biology identifies reproduction as a fundamental driver for living organisms, it stands to reason that if this focus is not realized, it might lead to a sense of unfulfillment. Women, like men, are deeply influenced by their biological wiring, and when the drive for motherhood is unfulfilled, they may seek meaning and satisfaction in other domains, such as careers in management, teaching, or entrepreneurship. As research highlights:

> *"Women working part-time, self-employed women, homemakers, and women on maternity leave are shown to have higher affective well-being than full-time employees".*

- **DOI:** 10.1007/s11150-021-09588-1

This underscores that well-being often thrives in roles that allow for a woman to have some sense of purpose, either in nurturing children, or contributing to the workplace in a less stressed fashion. Further into this study, women seem to be just as happy unemployed as they are employed, which is markedly different than how men experience a lack of employment.

In my experience working with women over the years, I've observed that while many find fulfillment in their careers before having children, this fulfillment often shifts once they become mothers. Some women feel less satisfied with work alone after experiencing the deep connection and purpose that motherhood can bring. However, many women still wish to work, and their individual needs and experiences can often be understood through frameworks like the Developmental Archetypes, hormonal health considerations, and societal influences.

This perspective is not to undermine the importance of women working if they desire or need to, but rather to highlight that, biologically speaking, motherhood often represents a profound and natural priority for many women. Recognizing this priority can help us better understand the interplay between personal fulfillment, work, and the biological design that shapes us.

However, imbalances arise when a woman doesn't feel fulfilled. A common example is the *babygirl* archetype, which stems from a lack of masculine integration. Women in this archetype may unconsciously project fatherly expectations onto their partners, calling them "daddy" as part of the dynamic (it is important to note that fulfilled women can still enjoy saying the term to their lovers). While this can be playful and fun, if rooted in unresolved needs, it risks perpetuating emotional voids for both partners. Interestingly, when paired with a *Manifestor* archetype, this dynamic can either amplify their unmet needs or serve as a path toward mutual healing.

Another scenario involves women who develop trauma from social rejection or perceived inferiority—perhaps due to physical differences, health ailments to induce neuroendocrinological susceptibility to anxiety, or ridicule during formative years. For instance, redheads might be more prone to developing anxiety-driven trauma, leading to feelings of inferiority.

"We confirmed that the intensity of hair redness negatively correlated with physical health, mental health, fecundity and sexual desire, and positively with the number of kinds of drugs prescribed by a doctor currently taken, and with reported symptoms of impaired mental health. It also positively correlated with certain neuropsychiatric disorders, most strongly with learning disabilities disorder and phobic disorder in men and general anxiety disorder in women."

- **PMID:** 31792316

These early experiences can shape their sense of sexual identity and attraction, sometimes driving them toward non-traditional relationship dynamics as a means of seeking safety.

Feelings of inferiority can have a profound impact, as I've personally experienced in my own struggles to connect with more feminine, sweet women in the past. These imbalances often highlight deeper emotional needs that, once addressed, can lead to growth and alignment.

Concluding Adult Fulfillment

Some of my statements may seem wild or even far-fetched, but they are rooted in my personal experiences and research. I approach these topics without bias, driven only by a genuine desire to share my story and the insights I've gained.

The Mother and Father

In my online premium group, I emphasize the importance of the individual on a date asking their potential lover one fundamental question: *What is their relationship like with their parents, and are they aware of the behaviors they've developed from it?*

This question is critical because much of the $28 billion-a-year behavioral therapy industry revolves around issues stemming from childhood upbringing. While most parents are doing their best, even the most well-intentioned efforts often fall short of providing an optimal environment.

Children need clear and polarized examples of masculinity and femininity. When even one parent fails to embody this polarity, the child often grows up without integrating those crucial examples. This imbalance profoundly influences what they are attracted to in relationships, as their unmet needs become a driving force behind their choices.

If a person isn't aware of their own behaviors and patterns, they're likely to project their unresolved traumas onto their romantic partners. In my perspective, the roles of father and mother are directly aligned with our romantic attractions. For a son, his mother sets the benchmark for his future partners, and the same goes for a daughter and her father.

To develop my system and help people in their relationships, I created an archetype framework that categorizes individuals based on these dynamics. At its core, this system begins with five foundational *Developmental Archetypes*, which I will outline further in my teachings.

The Developmental Archetypes

This archetype system has helped me reach new heights in dating and has guided my 1:1 clients to achieve profound success in their relationships. The Developmental Archetypes operate on an unconscious magnetic pull, where each person is drawn to what they are missing. These archetypes have been instrumental in aligning femininity and masculinity within individuals, fostering a deeper desire for the opposite sex and creating love-based, traditional relationships.

The five core archetypes serve as the foundation of the system, like the roots of a tree. From there, they branch into various subcategories, which will be introduced later, with early access provided through the premium group.

This system is built on the premise that the mind is divided into two aspects: feminine and masculine. The archetypes reflect this, with men and women who lean either into their masculine or feminine sides. The goal is to appreciate and integrate the imperfections in each archetype, offering hope for growth toward the *Balanced* archetype. From there, one can aspire to embody the radiant feminine woman or the emanating masculine man.

When I reference the roles of mother and father in this system, it's important to note that these terms represent examples of masculine and feminine energy rather than biological relationships. Even individuals without biological or adoptive parents can integrate these examples in other ways.

Keep in mind...

While upbringing often determines whether someone leans more masculine or feminine, I believe systemic bodily disturbances can anchor someone in a particular archetype, even if they've healed psychologically or spiritually. Neurodivergence, PCOS, and other endocrinological issues may influence how well someone fits into this archetype system.

For instance, someone with ADD/ADHD might display feminine traits due to the imbalance inherent in the condition, while those with ASD might exhibit hyper masculine traits as mentioned under the section ADD/ADHD & ASD. Women with PCOS often develop more masculine characteristics because of the increased production of male hormones caused by ovarian cysts.

Factors like heavy metals, synthetic chemicals, microbial overgrowth, and environmental disturbances often disrupt hormones, contributing to these imbalances. While these imbalances can push someone toward an archetype, they should be addressed for a more integrated and holistic sense of self.

Lastly, it's worth noting that earlier generations, such as those from and before Generation X, are less likely to experience these imbalances due to a stronger presence of traditional masculine and feminine examples in their societal frameworks. They may have also been less 'cognitively dissonant' and more open to taking on new role models passively.

The babygirl - Woman seeking the inner adult

Integrated: The mother, or chose to be more feminine

Yearning: The father, or male traits

Positives: Warm/nurturing, in-tune w/ emotions, soft and graceful, receptive/learns fast, playful

Negatives: Lacks boundaries, can be a bit of a doormat, naive judgment in relationships, feather in the wind, doesn't do conflict well, unrealistic idealism, lacks self worth.

Physical Associations: ADD/ADHD, PCOS, Estrogen dominance

The *babygirl* archetype is a woman who had a feminine example in her life and chose to integrate that example without suppressing her own femininity. However, she often yearns for the masculine due to a gap in her early life—a father who left, failed to lead, caused harm to her or others, or didn't provide the acknowledgment she needed. While she doesn't always harbor hatred or aversion toward men, she may struggle with trust, longing for the strength and presence of masculinity.

This archetype can form even without a specific upbringing and can simply result from a woman's natural orientation toward the feminine side of her mind.

The *babygirl* is sometimes labeled as a 'ship-jumper.' For example, if her partner loses his job, she may not have the resilience to tough it out alongside him. At the same time, her deep loyalty might compel her to stay regardless of hardship, highlighting the tension between her reliance on external stability and her innate devotion. She is prone to being a "doormat" by the intensely masculine men she is drawn to, or manipulated by intellectually inclined, feminine-leaning men who seek her out to compensate for their own shortcomings in masculinity.

She has the potential to learn competency—a role her father should have guided her through—and can become self-sufficient while still embodying her femininity. However, without a fully integrated father figure, she may develop an underlying ego and lack discernment when it comes to men. This poor judgment can manifest both in choosing partners and navigating relationships, as understanding what a man truly *is* and *feels like* is crucial for cultivating better relational patterns.

The Warrioress - Woman seeking the inner child

Integrated: The father, or chose to be more masculine

Yearning: The mother, or female traits

Positives: Competent, loyal, protective, rational, authentic, self-disciplined, purpose-driven

Negatives: Lacks vulnerability, controlling, too independent, prone to cynicism, lacks maternal connection

Physical Associations: ASD, Endometriosis, Bipolar, PCOS

The *Warrioress* archetype is one I'm deeply familiar with, as I used to only attract masculine women. Even now, they may still feel drawn to me, but I no longer feel the same pull unless they've discovered a deeper radiant femininity within themselves.

The *Warrioress* often stems from a strained relationship with her mother or from an internalized focus on the masculine side of her mind while subconsciously seeking to fill the voids left by what a feminine mother is supposed to provide. She may have experienced a mother who was absent, dismissive, or abusive. In these circumstances, her masculinity wasn't suppressed, leading her to find strength and solace in competency and action—orienting her world through *doing* rather than *being*.

She typically has male friends and understands men well, making her an excellent candidate for leadership roles, such as a manager, where she can balance natural feminine empathy with masculine decisiveness. This balance is most evident in *Warrioresses* who had a good father figure to guide them. However, not all women in this archetype had such a figure, and the absence or dysfunction of a father can greatly influence her expressions of this archetype. The absence of a father usually results in a girl becoming the *babygirl*, but life is nuanced.

Within the BDSM world, this archetype often manifests as the 'Mistress' or 'Dominatrix,' owing to her confidence in leading and commanding men. Her preferences in intimacy can sometimes reflect this dynamic, leaning toward more alternative or masculine forms of connection. However, many *babygirls* can be one, it's just in my experience that their style is much different and wasn't personally what I was seeking for myself. An example is that a dominant *babygirl* is more likely to have no desire to make a man better through shaping his competency. She is often oriented toward structureless pleasures and wouldn't mind having a good amount of 'financial domination' mixed in so she can do less work. Both archetypes charge for their services, but they generally handle the transactional aspects differently. The *Warrioress* is generally more transactional, though usually in a structured and clear way. The *Warrioress* is more likely to make this an entire career. The *babygirl* could often take money without any kind of structure to it, and is often biased in how she goes about charging someone. I never paid for my experiences, but I am aware that due to how many more sub men there are than the dominant women that men often have to pay.

A notable sub-archetype of the *Warrioress* is the *Valkyrie*. This version forms when a woman has a strong, positive connection with her masculine father (the masculine part is very important, because *Manifestor* fathers can also be well-loved by the daughter, and can often end up causing her to seek more masculine fulfillment than usual in relationships). The *Valkyrie* takes her purpose to another level by not only dominating or leading men but actively elevating them—becoming a kind of father figure in their lives. This adds a layer of nurturing guidance to her leadership, rooted in strength and purpose.

The Manifestor - Man seeking the inner adult

Integrated: The mother, or chose to be more feminine

Yearning: The father, or male traits

Positives: Empathetic, creative, intuitive, receiving, open-minded, can be purpose-driven

Negatives: Half truths and lies, potentially irrational, structureless, directionless, inconsistent, self-focused

Physical Associations: ADD/ADHD, Fatty liver/gallstones

The *Manifestor* archetype is one who primarily operates from the feminine side of his mind, often detaching from the physical world through daydreaming and introspection. He is highly empathetic, often identifying as an "empath," and may find his competency in creativity, whether through music, astrology, or other forms of artistic expression. Some sub-archetypes of the *Manifestor* have a sense of purpose that is frequently tied to serving others, often at the expense of themselves.

This man can either drown himself in the process of elevating others or lose himself in a life of whimsical expression. The masculine father figure he lacks—or the masculine he has yet to fully integrate—is meant to provide the balance that allows him to lift others while ensuring his own survival. His focus on people and purpose may originate from his own imagination or the influence of a strong feminine presence.

Men who identify with this archetype often share how the absence or resentment of a father figure has shaped their lives. For some, it manifests in an attraction to other men, with their desires rooted not in romance but in a subconscious search for the masculine traits they lacked growing up. This is just one potential reason why a *Manifestor* may find himself drawn to other men.

Additionally, this archetype is sometimes prone to becoming a submissive in relationships, especially to dominant women embodying the *Warrioress* archetype within the BDSM world. For me, overcoming this dynamic was part of the journey toward reclaiming my masculine side and breaking free from the desire to be dominated by such women.

⋮ The Forger - Man seeking the inner child

Integrated: The father, or chose to be more masculine

Yearning: The mother, or female traits

Positives: Strong, capable, reliable, structured, predictable, honest, protective

Negatives: Emotionally distant, inflexible, no/less fun, cynical, hard to please, less tolerance, sometimes a woman hater

Physical Associations: ASD, Bipolar

The *Forger* archetype often grapples with cerebral cynicism, frequently mistaken for "realism." He deeply values upfront honesty, disliking anything less, as it takes a touch of femininity to justify a half-truth. His communication can lack flow, but he is focused on getting the job done, often excelling as a problem solver and being quick to offer solutions. However, the depth of his ability to orient and connect with others depends heavily on his relationship with his mother, who ideally teaches this skill. A strained bond with her can leave him struggling to foster meaningful connections.

This man grew up leaning heavily on the masculine side of his mind, yearning deeply for the feminine as he matures. This yearning often stems from a mother who was absent, erratic, narcissistic, distant, abusive, or overly masculine. This can result in him potentially having large mood swings that seem uncontrollable.

He may thrive in demanding jobs and attract many women, but these realities come with challenges. His emotional absence can deprive a woman of the love she needs, or his overwhelming need for feminine energy may leave her drained. Feminine women are drawn to him, sensing both his wounds and his intense masculinity—a double-edged sword in their dynamic.

The *Forger* may struggle to bring out his playful side, often neglecting fun and games within a family setting. He's less likely to shamelessly dance or express himself freely. Yet, his longing for the feminine muse and her warmth often drives him toward creativity, such as producing music or finding other outlets for self-expression to release the suppressed side of his mind.

Despite his challenges, the *Forger* is reliable, real, and upfront. His honesty and high standards encourage those around him to rise to the occasion, shaping up in his presence. He can bring positive 'big brother' energy to others who need more masculine integration, like the *Manifestor* and *babygirl*.

The Balanced - Full integration

Integrated: The mother & father

Yearning: To give life

This archetype reflects full integration of the feminine mother and the masculine father, with strong bonds to both and active expression of each.

Men within this archetype are at the peak of competency as leaders. They inspire and guide with just enough vulnerability to connect deeply with others. They can be charismatic and funny but will confront disrespect directly and assertively.

Women in this archetype are equally balanced and dynamic. They embody nurturing qualities while maintaining a strong sense of assertiveness when necessary. They navigate social settings with ease, offering empathy and understanding while standing firm in their beliefs and values.

It's worth noting that this *Balanced* archetype does not include individuals with an "emanating masculine father" or a "radiant feminine mother." Those with such parents fall within this archetype but represent a unique and rare subcategory today.

The Imbalanced Balanced Sub - Archetype

I want to briefly cover a sub-archetype of the *Balanced* archetype.

This sub-archetype often exists because of physical health problems, such as mercury passing through the mother's placenta, infections like *Candida albicans* and *T. gondii* transferring to the next generation, or the use of phthalate-heavy makeup during pregnancy. The list goes on.

The characteristics for this archetype between men and women is very diverse depending on their state of health.

When health is compromised, identity can shift significantly due to hormonal dysfunction. Keep this in mind when considering these archetypes, as mentioned earlier.

Example of the Developmental Archetypes in Relationships

If a fairly wounded *Warrioress* were to date a fairly wounded *Forger*, it could quite possibly be the most volatile pairing of all the archetypes.

The way each archetype develops—shaped by their past examples and experiences—can significantly influence how the relationship functions. Regardless of these nuances, however, they are likely to face consistent conflict.

The *Warrioress* is less inclined to yield to vulnerability during an argument; the *Forger* is likely to do the same due to lacking the mother within him. She may stand her ground unwaveringly, presenting her case with such intensity that the *Forger*, overwhelmed, might retreat into a childlike version of himself. This reaction could stem from unresolved associations with an unpredictable or domineering maternal figure. On the other hand, the *Forger* prioritizes solutions and logical reasoning, as does the *Warrioress*. However, their shared focus on control and strategy can lead to frequent ego clashes over decision-making and parenting styles. These dynamics could result in recurring verbal disputes.

Despite their inherent challenges, these two core archetypes can achieve a semblance of harmony if they share a similar level of intelligence and align in their overarching values and goals—a rarity in today's world. They are capable of raising children who thrive in structured environments, particularly in workplace settings. However, without the mother nurturing warmth and sweetness within her feminine side, this pairing is likely to produce *Warrioress* daughters and *Forger* sons, perpetuating similar patterns in the next generation.

Concluding the Developmental Archetypes

These archetypes can be pretty exciting to get into, and I'm sure many of the readers may be saying that they're none of these, but know that they are **core** categories that **branch** outward into many **subcategories** that are not fully described in this book.

This is an example of the subcategory that is my specific sub archetype:

The Savior - Has a great feminine mother, strained relationship with the father

When a boy has a great mother, he often becomes oriented toward serving women with remarkable accomplishments. He's naturally drawn to a higher purpose that may seem grandiose. His innate ego as a man gives him the genuine belief that he can achieve it. Based on my own experience, it is entirely possible for him to dream and manifest himself to that level.

The core archetype at play here is the *Manifestor*. In my case, my focus was on healing the world and saving everyone—at the cost of drowning in the process.

It wasn't until I integrated the masculine side of my mind that I moved beyond this state of perpetual servitude. Now, I ensure I serve myself just enough to stay afloat, allowing me to help others without losing myself in the process.

***

A strained relationship with the father figure often compounds this dynamic. The mother appears as though she sits atop a mountain, unreachable, while no man seems capable of scaling high enough to meet her. This, combined with the boy's tendency to push his father away, frequently makes him critical of men and reluctant to integrate them into his life. His sense of brotherhood weakens as he dissociates from masculine men, leaning instead into feminine traits. He models himself after his mother while gaining little to no competency or structure from his father.

These archetypes represent snapshots of identity, and they can be transformed through improved health—I've done it myself. We'll explore these archetypes in greater depth in the premium group, with some of the content shared for free elsewhere. The ultimate goal is to seek to achieve the *Balanced* archetype and embody the radiant feminine or the emanating masculine. However, it's important to acknowledge that not everyone may reach this stage in their lifetime, and that's okay. Every archetype can bring great value as they are.

Even now, I have a *Manifestor* man, Brian Kuenning, helping me fill the gaps of this book. I also have a *Warrioress* named Geraecka Lyonns ensuring that I'm putting in enough effort and creating the impact this book is meant to make. My mother, a *Balanced* archetype, is able to offer unique contributions to the book such as what you the reader might **feel** when reading it, or general structuring of sentences and grammar. Each archetype has its own unique strengths, but I want the reader to understand that we can all seek greater balance and become more.

Concluding Development

Our formative years in life are absolutely crucial to proper psychological—and I argue endocrinological as well—development. Much of the traumatic events we experience today happen during our formative years, so we must give much more importance to upbringing if we want to achieve more balance in the world in which we live. A masculine man and a feminine woman reaching fulfillment prior to procreation is an ideal that I hope comes to fruition someday, so both parents are prepared to raise optimal children, and the children are then able to live lives as they are intended to.

Brotherhood & Sisterhood

When it comes to social dynamics, there's a powerful difference in the way men and women connect with one another. Women naturally form bonds with other women, and men with other men. However, these dynamics can become distorted if there are mixed hormonal influences within the groups.

It's okay to have one or two men in a brotherhood who lean more feminine-minded, but if the majority of the men share this mindset, the group dynamic can quickly shift into something more unproductive. In such a group, the men may not challenge each other or hold one another accountable in a masculine way. Instead, the interactions may become indirect, with a tendency to gossip or undermine each other's progress. Even when they try to be blunt or honest, their approach often lacks the strength and clarity that direct masculine confrontation brings. This creates a space where the energy isn't directed toward building each other up, but rather becoming stagnant or even toxic.

On the flip side, when women form groups where the majority lean masculine, it can bring its own set of problems. While these groups might have less interpersonal drama on the surface, they can easily develop a negative, judgmental tone, which often manifests as man-hating or disparagement. The women in such groups might feel empowered in the moment, but over time, this energy can seep into their personal lives, impacting their relationships and overall sense of well-being.

Both men and women need to be mindful of the balance in their groups. It's about the energy each individual brings into the dynamic, and how that either supports or detracts from the group's overall growth. Ideally, the balance of masculine and feminine energies in these groups should reflect the natural flow and needs of each individual, without leaning too heavily in one direction. When that balance is achieved, these dynamics can create spaces for real personal growth and authentic connection.

Optimal Brotherhood

A key realization from my experience in creating a brotherhood was the importance of physicality over intellectual discussions. While I brought together a group of intellectual types, none of us were anywhere near peak masculinity. Intellectual conversations and board games, though stimulating, kept us from tapping into our primal needs as men. I believe it's okay to have these kinds of men in a brotherhood, but they shouldn't dominate the group.

Brotherhood needs to be rooted in physical activities. Men thrive when they engage in activities that challenge them physically—things that push their bodies to their limits. These activities need to have a competitive or fitness-oriented edge. While it's perfectly fine to have intellectual conversations or play games now and then, they can't be the focus, as they only serve to further distance the group from healthy masculine integration.

One thing I noticed was that the men in the group—not all of them—exhibited feminine traits in ways that were unbalanced. This included things like deception, reactivity, and using underhanded tactics in arguments or when solving problems within the community. Masculine men are direct. They prefer face-to-face confrontation, addressing problems head-on with logic, merit, and integrity. In contrast, when men are less grounded in their masculinity, they can resort to emotional responses, deflecting from logical debate and making arguments more about feelings than facts.

True brotherhood, as I've come to understand, is about lifting each other up, challenging each other, and holding one another accountable. It's about finding solutions through merit, helping each other grow, and supporting each other through challenges. If one man stumbles, the others come to his aid, not out of pity but out of respect for his potential.

A brotherhood of men like this prevents the need for women to take on masculine responsibilities within a relationship. If a relationship falls into this imbalance, where the man is carrying the entire burden of responsibility, it becomes unsustainable. A man needs his brotherhood to lean on, not just his partner, in order to truly show up as his best self.

Chemical Benefits

Mentioned below are some hormonal benefits that men gain from having a *brotherhood*.

Oxytocin - bonding and trust

Dopamine - motivation and reward

Endorphins - stress relief and pleasure

Serotonin - mood stability

Testosterone - confidence and drive

Reduced *cortisol* - stress management

Prolactin - empathy and nurturing

GABA - relaxation and calm

Optimal Sisterhood

*The Optimal Sisterhood content is the written opinion of **Sara Whipp**, a polarity and relationships coach. Please note that she has not taken part in the rest of the book, so the book itself may not fully apply to her views.*

"When a woman begins leaning into her femininity for the first time, the biggest pushback often comes from her masculinized female friends, who feel confronted by her newfound softness and respect for the masculine. It's not uncommon for her to experience a complete restructuring of her social circle during this period.

Rejecting radical feminism and stepping away from the feminist tribe can feel overwhelming and scary. Daring to love and respect men, while embracing the inherent and pronounced differences between men and women, may lead to feelings of isolation and being cast out.

One of the most important steps she can take is to seek out a group of women on the same journey—women who are returning to feminine womanhood, opting out of the battle of the sexes, and focusing on becoming women of character. These women are dedicated to restoring the union between the masculine and feminine.

In an optimal sisterhood, we work side by side in devotion to our higher calling rather than sitting face to face gossiping, complaining, or tearing down men for sport.

Some of the most sacred connections I've found are with women devoted to the restoration of feminine womanhood. These women, instead of seeing others as competition, seek collaboration and create forward momentum in the movement toward union, respect for men, and a return to their innate femininity.

These women are coming home—not only to their physical dwellings but also to their own feminine essence. They inspire other women to do the same and encourage men to reclaim their masculinity.

This is the healing our culture desperately needs. This is the new sisterhood, and every woman is welcome here as we pioneer the path back home."

Chemical Benefits

The chemical benefits for *sisterhood* are nearly the same as for men, it's just that they benefit from positive associations with estrogen levels and balance vs. men and their increased testosterone.

Imbalanced Femininity & Masculinity

Recognizing when feminine and masculine traits become excessive is crucial, as this imbalance can create challenges. Identifying these imbalances is essential not only in relationships but in all areas of life.

Imbalanced Feminine Traits

The Tempest: Heightened sensitivity resulting in unpredictable mood swings, manipulation, or overreaction to small stressors.

The Clinging Vine: Relying on others for all forms of decision-making, lacking personal agency or initiative, leading to helplessness or codependency.

The Fragile Mirror: An intensified focus on self-worth through external validation, resulting in a fragile self-image.

The People-Pleaser: An excessive need to please others, leading to self-sacrifice and lack of boundaries.

The Eternal Sacrifice: An inclination to take on suffering or burdens, often unnecessarily, to feel valued or maintain relationships.

Imbalanced Masculine Traits

The Steamroller: An overbearing need to dominate or control others, sometimes manifesting as authoritarianism or a lack of empathy. This can in some ways be driven by fear, which leans more feminine.

The Silent Rock: Extreme stoicism to the point of detachment, avoiding emotional expression and creating distance from others.

The Lonely Pioneer: A refusal to ask for or accept help, resulting in isolation, burnout, or an inability to cooperate.

The Rigid Perfectionist: An intense focus on standards, leading to unrealistic expectations of oneself and others and an inability to accept imperfections.

The Chained Gladiator: Viewing everything as a challenge to be won, leading to relentless ambition, aggression, or inability to connect.

Concluding Proposed Hypothesis and Perspective - Psychology

Our mental health is profoundly shaped by external events, which directly influence us on a physiological level. Walking the path toward polarity demands a top-down approach, integrating psychological principles such as identifying our imbalances, using archetypes to uncover specific gaps left by the mother and father, and recognizing the essence of a radiant feminine woman or an emanating masculine man.

However, polarity isn't confined to psychology alone. It extends beyond into the broader realms of science and lived experiences, offering a multifaceted perspective on achieving balance.

Proposed Hypothesis and Perspective - Physiology

Hormones

Without getting overly complicated with how hormones chemically operate, men primarily have more 'androgens' (male hormones, testosterone is the main androgen) than women, and women will have more 'estrogens' (female hormones). It is important for men and women to know that both sexes have male and female hormones.

For those who resist being labeled as 'male' or 'female,' simply observing the contributions and behaviors of each within the human system—regardless of biological sex—will provide a clear understanding of their respective roles.

Androgens in **men** support the development of the male reproductive system, secondary sexual characteristics, regulation of libido, maintenance of muscle mass, strength, bone density and growth, mood, and cognitive function. Androgens in **women** support libido, bone strength, muscle mass, energy levels, mood stability, and hormonal balance through their conversion into estrogens.

Estrogens in **women** support the development of the female reproductive system, regulation of the menstrual cycle, maintenance of secondary sexual characteristics, bone density, cardiovascular health, and emotional well-being. Estrogens in **men** support bone health, regulate libido, aid in sperm maturation, maintain cardiovascular function, and balance mood and cognitive function.

Beyond the basics, estradiol (E2), the most powerful female hormone, is necessary for male sexual activity and reproduction. This is important because many men believe that it's just testosterone that drives their virility. Testosterone is important, but without estradiol, it would not function as it should, and the same applies to the consistency of their semen.

On the other side of the coin, testosterone, the most powerful male hormone, supports sexual desire and sense of well-being in females.

Hormones are incredibly facinating, to say the least, but cannot function without the mineral system.

Minerals

In the realm of minerals and ionomics, Dr. Hans Selye, Dr. Eck, and Dr. Lawrence Wilson have been pioneers in exploring how minerals operate within the human system, particularly through the use of hair tissue mineral analysis (HTMA). While this practice has gained more popularity recently, it has long been a method for those seeking alternative health approaches. Mineral balancing is a concept where individuals work to adjust the minerals in their system to displace heavy metals and find a relative mineral homeostasis.

Masculine & Feminine Minerals

Dr. Eck, in particular, proposed that copper was a feminine mineral, while zinc was masculine in nature. Similarly, copper makes iron more efficient, where men have more iron in their system than women. A mineral balancing practitioner I've known for years had mentioned that iron can be seen as a male counterpart to copper, just as zinc is. In polarized relationships the woman will often be a big part of what makes a man better through her inspiration, as copper does similar with iron. Interestingly, copper may be one of the key elements responsible for me writing this book, especially when we break it down chemically.

I personally experienced a profound shift when a portion of my beard turned bright red, practically overnight. This was in 2021, and it felt like a rebirth—a moment of newfound masculine willpower and hormones. In hindsight, I believe this transformation was the result of my body unloading biounavailable copper (though there's a small chance it was mercury) that I had no idea I was carrying. Since then, my life has been a whirlwind of intense circumstances and manifestations, which I can't fully encapsulate in this book—perhaps another time.

But the key point is this: copper and zinc have much more significant effects on our endocrine systems and physiology than we often recognize.

There are numerous studies linking zinc sufficiency with testosterone production and copper with estrogen. This relationship is well-established at this point.

Biounavailable Copper

The concept of 'bio-unavailable copper' is relatively newer, but has been embraced for some time by HTMA practitioners familiar with Dr. Eck's work. While some people may advocate for copper supplementation beyond the typical 2 mg per day, it's important to differentiate between supplemental copper and biounavailable copper. I believe some individuals may unintentionally create imbalances by supplementing with too much copper, thinking it will boost mood or emotional depth, given copper's association with feminine energy. Bioavailable copper, on the other hand, can displace biounavailable copper, contributing to a more balanced system. So it's hard to say just how much is too much.

An example regarding biounavailable copper is that the copper in a copper IUD is designed to act locally in the uterus to prevent fertilization and implantation, meaning it releases copper in the form of ionic copper into the uterine cavity. While this copper is intended to stay in the uterus, some of it can enter the bloodstream and other tissues. However, ionic copper released in this manner may not be bioavailable or easily absorbed by the body because it's not in the form that can be readily utilized by cells. Instead, it may accumulate in places where it does not contribute to critical biochemical functions. Thus, potentiating biounavailability.

Another example, and this is my hypothesis, is when the immune system identifies an opportunistic pathogen like *Candida albicans* (the overgrowth of systemic yeast I experienced), it can often attempt to utilize copper to poison the yeast. In some cases, however, this effort can fail, potentially rendering the copper biounavailable.

Zinc

Zinc is particularly fascinating. When taken at the right times and doses, as determined through HTMA, zinc can not only help eliminate bio-unavailable copper but also support the sodium-to-potassium ratio (Na/K) by raising potassium and making sodium more efficient. Keep in mind that zinc can lower sodium, so going too far can negatively impact the Na/K ratio. This ratio, in Dr. Wilson's terms, represents life and purpose. A balanced Na/K ratio is often seen as a marker of vitality and direction.

Minerals are truly fascinating, and as research continues, we're increasingly seeing that minerals precipitate into hair tissue based not just on diet or heavy metal exposure, but on the external factors that influence an individual's life. When external influences—such as upbringing—go awry or lose alignment, HTMA testing reveals an impact on mineral homeostasis and can suggest a lot about cognitive development.

Minerals are one of the most fundamental components of the human system, and they play an essential role in endocrine function.

The Microbiome

Microbiology is one of the most underexplored areas of science, despite being a significant factor in our identities and overall endocrine health. There is much left to be discovered in this field. The microbiome, essentially an ecosystem within our bodies, extends well beyond the gastrointestinal tract (GIT).

For generations, the medical community largely believed that the microbiome was confined to the GIT. However, it has since become clear that these trillions of microbes inhabit virtually every part of our bodies, from head to toe.

While the reader may now be more familiar with the influence of copper on estrogen, zinc on testosterone, and the roles these hormones play in defining female and male traits, have you heard of the 'microgenderome'? This scientific term wasn't even recognized by ChatGPT back in 2023 when I had asked its opinion of it, though interestingly, Bard was familiar with it.

Research into the microgenderome is still in its infancy and remains largely unexplored. However, enough data exists to raise important questions to connect it to existing research in related fields.

One key observation is that certain microbes in the microbiome are no longer as prevalent today as they were 40+ years ago. *Limosilactobacillus reuteri* is one such microbe, and based on current research, it stands out as one of the most crucial bacteria for supporting both immune and hormonal health in both males and females.

L. reuteri for men: Boosts testosterone production, which enhances masculine traits like increased muscle mass, height, testicular size, and deeper voice. It also supports overall gut health and mental well-being, influencing male social dominance and behavior.

L. reuteri for women: Helps balance estrogen levels and supports vaginal health by maintaining an acidic environment, reducing the risk of infections like bacterial vaginosis. Its effect on oxytocin may also support maternal behavior and bonding.

So, why are some specialists stating that certain beneficial microbes are disappearing in large percentages among modern humans?

Take *Limosilactobacillus reuteri* as an example—Dr. Davis claims that it has been lost by 96% of modern Americans.

The likely reasons for this are complex, but *L. reuteri* is highly susceptible to factors like antibiotics, chronic stress, grain-heavy and yeast-forming diets, mold-laden gastrointestinal tracts and bloodstreams, heavy metal toxicity, and potentially much more.

Personally, I believe that taking an entire bottle of *L. reuteri* at one time may have played a significant role in my own masculinization.

Prior to the dry fast that changed everything for me hormonally, I took an entire bottle of L. reuteri. However, this was not likely the sole factor, as mentioned earlier...

It's also important to consider other beneficial microbes that play crucial roles in the health of our microbiome, as these can significantly impact our overall well-being:

Lactobacillus gasseri

Men: This species helps manage weight, especially by reducing visceral fat, which can boost testosterone levels and overall metabolic health. It also has a hand in gut-brain communication, sharpening mental focus, and improving mood.

Women: For women, L. gasseri helps with weight loss and hormonal balance, particularly reducing belly fat tied to estrogen dominance or PCOS. It also plays a big role in vaginal health, preventing yeast infections and UTIs.

Bifidobacterium bifidum

Men: This one keeps the gut healthy, influencing testosterone by lowering inflammation and oxidative stress that translates to higher fertility, better energy, and overall health.

Women: B. bifidum is great for balancing the immune system and helping with estrogen metabolism. It aids in menstrual regularity and can ease PMS symptoms, improving mood along the way.

Lactobacillus crispatus

Men: Even though it's mostly beneficial for women, men still get immune support and a healthier gut environment from L. crispatus.

Women: This species is a key player in the vaginal microbiome, maintaining a healthy acidic pH to ward off infections like bacterial vaginosis and yeast. It also helps balance estrogen and supports overall reproductive health.

Lactobacillus rhamnosus

Men: It's all about the gut-brain axis here - L. rhamnosus helps with mood and anxiety regulation, making social interactions smoother and reducing stress-related testosterone dips. It also keeps the gut in check for better hormonal balance.

Women: In women, it prevents UTIs and promotes healthy vaginal flora. Plus, it helps regulate mood during hormonal swings, like those from the menstrual cycle or menopause.

Bifidobacterium longum

Men: This species helps cut down on inflammation, supports heart health, and indirectly keeps testosterone levels in check by improving gut health and lowering stress.

Women: It helps with digestion and metabolism, key players in hormone and estrogen balance. It's also tied to better skin health, especially with hormonal acne.

Akkermansia muciniphila

Men: This one improves metabolic health, which helps keep testosterone levels up by cutting body fat. It also strengthens the gut barrier, helping men maintain energy, especially when stressed.

Women: For women, it supports weight management and insulin sensitivity, reducing estrogen dominance. It also benefits fertility and mood by balancing overall gut and hormonal health.

Lactobacillus plantarum

<u>Men</u>: L. plantarum is great for lowering inflammation, aiding muscle recovery, and improving gut health, which can help maintain testosterone levels by reducing chronic stress.

<u>Women</u>: In women, it supports digestion, helps balance estrogen, reduces bloating, and stabilizes mood through gut health.

Lactobacillus casei

<u>Men</u>: This strain regulates the immune system, improving recovery from illness or stress, which helps keep testosterone steady. It also supports digestion and nutrient absorption.

<u>Women</u>: It aids in digestion and fights inflammation, helping with conditions like endometriosis or PCOS. Plus, it's known to reduce anxiety and support mental health.

Bifidobacterium breve

<u>Men</u>: B. breve helps metabolize fat, cutting body fat, and keeping testosterone optimal. It also reduces inflammation and improves overall metabolic health.

<u>Women</u>: It aids in weight management and estrogen metabolism, reducing PMS symptoms or hormone-driven skin issues. It also supports mental clarity and mood regulation during hormonal changes.

A note to the reader, do keep in mind that just putting probiotics in any human system's gastrointestinal tract doesn't always equate to these benefits, as many probiotics are already dead prior to sale, die before arrival, on arrival, or at some point soon after. Probiotics are a fickle aspect to alternative health, and this is where getting a gut health professional involved can help a lot.

The Sympathetic (SNS) & Parasympathetic (PNS) Nervous Systems

I believe the sympathetic and parasympathetic nervous systems align with masculine and feminine energies based on their core functions and characteristics.

Sympathetic Nervous System

The sympathetic nervous system thrives in moments where strength and clarity are essential. It's about taking action, setting boundaries, and maintaining structure in the face of challenges. This system, much like masculine energy, is designed to protect and provide, ensuring survival through focus and determination. However, just like a man stuck in his masculine energy for too long without balance, the sympathetic system can become overworked. When it dominates for extended periods, it leads to burnout and rigidity, leaving little room for recovery or introspection.

Women, often caught in prolonged fight-or-flight states due to stress, can experience significant long-term health consequences. Chronic activation of the sympathetic system in women has been linked to hormonal imbalances and adrenal fatigue, often exacerbated by workplace demands or societal pressures. Men are not immune to this, as they, too, can hit the wall of adrenal fatigue. However, women seem to encounter these health impacts more frequently in my observations, likely because their bodies are more sensitive to stress-related hormonal shifts.

The sympathetic system is not inherently harmful—it plays a vital role in resilience and action. But like all things, it must work in harmony with its counterpart, the parasympathetic system. Without moments of rest and softness, even the most resilient systems will eventually wear down.

Parasympathetic Nervous System

The parasympathetic nervous system mirrors feminine energy. It's the force that slows things down, focuses on internal balance, and allows for recovery. This system takes over when the body needs rest, guiding it into repair mode by lowering the heart rate and supporting digestion. It's not about pushing forward or reacting to threats but about creating a sense of calm and safety wherein the body can regroup and heal. When everything around feels stable, the parasympathetic system ensures that energy is used to maintain health and prepare for future challenges.

Feminine energy, like the parasympathetic system, isn't built for confrontation or external conflict. It thrives in stillness and care, supporting growth and restoration. But too much of this energy without the counterbalance of action can leave someone overly passive, unable to step up when it's necessary to face challenges. Balance is key—knowing when to lean into calm and when to activate strength is what keeps both systems in check.

Looking back, my life as a kid and young adult felt dominated by this parasympathetic pull to an almost dysfunctional degree. I was stuck in a state of stillness and low energy, where doing anything felt like pushing through a fog. Things started to shift for me when I discovered coffee. For the first time, my brain fog lifted, and I became sharp, confident, and capable of taking on anything I set my mind to. It took me years to understand what was happening—how caffeine was engaging my sympathetic nervous system and compensating for what felt like an imbalance in my body. In hindsight, it makes perfect sense why coffee felt like a lifeline, especially as I later pieced together its impact on ADD and ADHD.

Concluding Defining Polarity

Now that we've highlighted some of the key arguments for why 'polarity' has merit based in reality, it's important to acknowledge that there's much more evidence proving its existence beyond what I've shared here.

Taking both a psychological and physiological approach to polarity is essential for reaching that peak state of being, one that brings an unmistakable experience both for the individual and those they connect with. It's truly beautiful, and I can say that from personal experience after unlocking a significant portion of my own potential.

At one point in my journey, I discovered that much of what I had desired from the women in my past was almost entirely centered around my endocrine system. Much of what I should have received from health and upbringing was instead concentrated in my sexual experience—an experience profoundly influenced by my hormones and minerals, but ultimately marked by a sense of unfulfilled longing.

POLARITY
BASICS

Polarity Basics: Health

Our health is everything. Without optimal physical health, optimal psychological health cannot truly exist.

The focus of *Polarity Basics: Health* is to guide readers in identifying root issues that may be affecting their lives, particularly when questioning why they aren't polarized on a physical level. Building on my explanation of systems science, the following provides a basic overview of what constitutes a 'disturbance' within the human system.

The content that follows is not exhaustive and should only be seen as a basic framework for understanding polarity in terms of health.

Antibiotics & Diet

To understand how antibiotics have disrupted hormonal balance over the past decade, we need to examine their deeper impact on human health. The essential microbes highlighted in the Microbiome section—organisms critical to maintaining our body's systems—are not just diminished but can be wiped out by antibiotics, some almost permanently, such as Limosilactobacillus reuteri.

A study involving over 12,000 children revealed a striking outcome: neonatal antibiotic exposure within the first 14 days of life significantly reduced boys' **weight**, **height**, and **BMI** up to age six. Interestingly, this effect was absent in girls, which makes me think of bacteria like L. reuteri that are often sex-biased. These findings are a wake-up call, especially considering the decades-long overuse of antibiotics in pediatric care. The irony? Many of the dietary habits—like excessive sugar consumption—that often drive the need for antibiotics through insulin resistance that leads to poor immunity, only compound the problem.

Diet is an often overlooked cornerstone of immune health. While the push by influential figures toward lifestyle and dietary changes is a step forward, even these advocates frequently resort to antibiotics when faced with clinical challenges. I've seen this firsthand, working with clients who turned to me after exhausting traditional approaches, often viewing me as a last resort.

Online, many are questioning why reducing sugar intake has become a cornerstone for improving immune health. For those following a carnivore diet, the benefits are even more apparent. I believe this is because the diet directly targets the microbes that complicate immune health daily—microbes that rely on glucose to survive and proliferate. By cutting out sugar, one is essentially starving these microbes, allowing the immune system to regain its balance. This reduction in sugar helps eliminate the fuel for harmful bacteria, fungi, and parasites, letting the body focus on maintaining a healthy, thriving immune system. This level of immunity can potentially help someone to be able to fight off infections naturally. I know this worked for me when I beat bacterial meningitis one winter with dry fasting and diet.

The notion that the microbiome fully recovers in six months to two years is a widespread belief, even among natural health practitioners promoting optimal diets. While partial recovery is possible, emerging research suggests that some vital bacterial species may never return to their original state.

As the 12,000+ children study noted:

> "Thus, we conclude that neonatal antibiotic exposure is associated with a long-term gut microbiome perturbation and **may result in reduced growth in boys during the first six years of life** while antibiotic use later in childhood is associated with increased body mass index."

- doi.org/10.1038/s41467-020-20495-4

This isn't a crusade against antibiotics—they have their place. But understanding their potential to harm long-term health is vital. The ripple effects of their use have only grown since Sir Alexander Fleming's discovery of Penicillin in the 1920s. It's worth noting that this first antibiotic was derived from Penicillium, a mold that produces toxic byproducts known as mycotoxins.

Here's what exposure to mycotoxins from Penicillium chrysogenum can look like:

Ochratoxin A

- Linked to kidney damage, potentially contributing to chronic kidney disease over time.

- Classified as a possible human carcinogen, with mounting evidence pointing to its role in kidney cancer.

- Suppresses immune function, leaving individuals more susceptible to infections—a particular concern for those with pre-existing health issues.

- May have neurotoxic effects, though additional studies are needed to confirm the extent of this risk.

Patulin

- Causes gastrointestinal issues such as nausea, vomiting, and abdominal pain.

- While evidence is less robust compared to other mycotoxins, patulin may also suppress immune function.

Concluding Antibiotics & Diet

The widespread belief that Penicillin is "safe and effective" overlooks its nuanced effects on the microbiome. While I'm not claiming that antibiotics directly replicate the symptoms of mycotoxins, their disruption of essential bacteria is undeniable—especially those critical to maintaining hormonal equilibrium.

Antibiotics derived from fungi often excel at halting bacterial overgrowth, yet they are far from a universal solution. Classes of antibiotics like the quinolones are much different than Penicillin, each bringing its own mechanisms of action and unique risks. An antibiotic's origin and class matter profoundly in determining its impact—not just on the infection being treated, but on the body's broader balance of health.

One man I know who was given Ciprofloxacin (Cipro) ended up losing much of his mobility and nearly all of his weight. He was an athletic man with decent health too. Cipro falls within the fluoroquinolone antibiotic class of drugs. On online forums, it commonly harms people long term, where group members have come up with the statement, "I've been floxed." It breaks my heart to see this happen, and what is worse is that it's still prescribed despite the possible setbacks.

Do your own research when it comes to antibiotics!

Fungi

To extend the discussion on fungi and their impact on human health, there are many opportunistic species that can grow out of control. Generally, these fungi fall into two categories that affect internal human systems: yeast and mold. Dermatophytes also count, but they are primarily surface tissue dwellers and aren't the primary focus of this book and its focus on hormonal health.

While the fungi mentioned may not always directly lead to hormonal disruptions, they can certainly have an indirect effect on hormonal health.

It's important to note that, although the focus here will be on opportunistic fungi, some fungi, like *Saccharomyces*, can actually be supportive.

Fungi - Yeast

The most prolific yeast in the modern world is *Candida*, specifically *Candida albicans*. This is the species I had an overgrowth of at birth, and at some point during adolescence, it developed into a systemic infection.

Some species of *Candida*, like *C. auris*, are particularly dangerous and often claim the lives of those infected. This species thrives primarily in sanitary, nosocomial environments where there is little bacterial competition. It typically grows due to the inappropriate use of antibiotics.

Candida albicans is the much more common species that affects many people in the modern world. Those who have taken antibiotics, suffered from chronic stress, eaten a poor diet, inherited it from their parents, or experienced heavy metal toxicity and environmental disruptions to immune health are particularly vulnerable.

> *"Candida is the most common human fungal pathogen and the cause of invasive candidiasis, the fourth leading cause of nosocomial bloodstream infection in the United States with an estimated annual cost of ~US$2 billion and mortality that exceeds 40% despite administration of antifungal therapy in modern intensive care unit facilities."*

- doi.org/10.1371/journal.ppat.1003079

Fungi - Mold

As far as molds are concerned, their pathogenesis (their ability to cause disease) is primarily linked to what the mold is feeding on and the mycotoxins it introduces into the host. These toxins often target organs like the kidneys and liver. Molds have become a significant problem today because they can keep individuals in a persistent state of immune compromise, making recovery extremely challenging. Various mycotoxins are known to disrupt reproductive health by creating imbalances in estrogen and androgen levels, altering hormone metabolism due to liver compromise, and even mimicking estrogen.

Fungi - Deep Dive on Yeast

What many people don't know about yeast, is that Candida is quite skilled at mimicking our tissue to evade the immune system. I hypothesize this is connected to pathologies like endometriosis, PCOS, EDS, various forms of cancer, and likely much more, but this requires further research.

Yeasts are also capable of resisting the body's attempts to poison them with copper. Sometimes, this is done through phagocytosis, where a macrophage—a white blood cell (WBC)—essentially engulfs the yeast and then draws copper in to poison it. However, this process can fail, resulting in the WBC's death.

Candida can also enter a more virulent hyphal state, which allows it to colonize areas of the body more effectively. It uses the host's estrogen to facilitate this. My suspicion is that the copper intended to kill the Candida, when it inevitably becomes biounavailable in the system, may contribute to a mineral imbalance that can eventually lead to a hormonal imbalance.

This imbalance can potentially increase estrogen production or impair estrogen metabolism in the liver, encouraging more hyphal transitions of the yeast for further colonization. Reactive oxygen species (ROS) from the inflammation of tissues that produce estrogen (such as those containing aromatase enzymes) can also potentially upregulate estrogen production in the body.

When all of this is considered, the hormonal havoc that can ensue may alter the way a person thinks—and even what they're attracted to.

There is much more to Candida and other yeasts, but it isn't entirely relevant to the point of the book.

Fungi - Deep Dive on Mold

Once upon a time, around the age of 10, I got Bell's Palsy from toilet mold. Yeah, toilet mold. A huge fuzzy round and bulging spore was found underneath the bathroom, visible in the garage below.

Beyond the unusual nature of mold being that toxic, there's more to it than meets the eye. Did you know that mold can disrupt the menstrual cycle and make it irregular? That it can lower testosterone, not just through raised cortisol, but through other mechanisms as well? That it can cause low muscle mass and severe fatigue? Mold is certianly a serious problem.

Something else important to understand on a broader scale is that the majority of citric acid on the market comes from mold excretions, often grown on corn. What's being used isn't fruit extracts to preserve food, but a substance known to disrupt bacterial colonies.

"Citric acid, an organic acid with bactericidal ability, has an antibacterial mechanism that mainly involves disrupting the cell membrane of bacteria and lowering the pH to arrest bacterial growth. Citric acid as a food additive is not natural citric acid; it is manufactured through fermentation using Aspergillus niger. Approximately 99% of the world's production of manufactured citric acid has been carried out using the fungus Aspergillus niger since 1919."

- PMID: 37240435 & **PMID:** 30128297

There is limited research into the contraindications of citric acid, but I do believe it can pose a potentially serious problem if consumed on a regular basis.

Another notable concern is the mycotoxin zearalenone (ZEA) produced by the mold genus Fusarium.

> *"In summary, our data suggest ZEA acts as an antagonist in endometriotic tissue when estrogen is sufficient but turns to estrogenic activity in the absence of estrogen in the development of endometriosis. ZEA also inhibits ectopic tissue growth by inhibiting the inflammatory response in the endometriosis model."*

*- **PMID:** 36068753*

Remember the connection I made earlier in the book regarding high stress and pregnenolone being utilized for cortisol production as a priority? When the estrogen to progesterone ratio is compromised, it can potentially lead to endometriosis. ZEA's ability to mimic estrogen is a serious problem and can contribute to numerous health issues in an individual.

Concluding Fungi

Fungi were my first foray into alternative health, and of all the topics I've researched in epidemiology, it is certainly fungi and its fascinating means of survival in the human host system that I have studied the most. There is still so much more to research about fungi, to the point that I wonder if fungi were to take just one more step in adaptation to mammalian biology, could they do to us what Ophiocordyceps does to ants? They can take over the motor controls of ants with their mycotoxins because ants only have nerve clusters for brains. Imagine if our immune systems were rocked harder and harder as each year passes, and more and more yeast and fungi grow out of control, invading new areas of the body. Scary thought, right? Not likely, though. Still, we should probably take our societal health seriously, just in case there are people who don't want to become fungus zombies or have to fight them. Haha.

Parasites

Parasites living within us is a scary thought, but it's a very real reality, even in the most sanitary environments. It's almost certain that parasites will colonize people who have ever owned animals. Parasites are categorically similar to fungi in that they also fall into three broad categories that colonize humans: protozoa (single-celled organisms), helminths (worms/flukes), and ectoparasites (surface dwellers). As with our approach to fungi, we will refrain from exploring the surface colonizers.

Similar to fungi, some parasites can actually be pretty benign and may even support the host. However, there are no known parasites that are required for optimal human health, as some bacteria are. While many parasites colonize humans, I want to focus on the ones I've found to be the most troublesome.

But why do parasites have any connection to polarity and relationships? Don't worry, I'll get to that part...

Helminths

Strongyloides stercoralis, a helminthic parasite, stands out due to its ability to persist in the human host indefinitely through an "auto infecting" lifecycle. Unlike many parasites that require transmission via external environments, Strongyloides can complete its life cycle within a single host, evading elimination for decades.

"In immunocompromised individuals, it can present with severe symptoms, hyperinfection, or disseminated disease. Reported mortality in cases of disseminated Strongyloidiasis is 87.1%."

- PMID: 37954715

"Observations suggest that Strongyloides stercoralis may be a relevant co-factor in HTLV-1-related T cell lymphomas."

- PMID: 27956028

Why Strongyloides Is a Major Concern

The unique biology of Strongyloides makes it a formidable parasite. Acquired through contaminated water, food, or direct skin contact with infected soil, the infection often begins with minimal symptoms or even remains asymptomatic. However, its ability to evade immune detection and continuously reproduce within the host poses significant challenges for eradication.

Immunocompromised

In individuals with compromised immune systems—such as those undergoing chemotherapy, taking corticosteroids, or living with HIV/AIDS—the parasite can multiply unchecked, leading to **hyperinfection syndrome** or disseminated disease. These severe manifestations can result in widespread tissue damage, immune dysregulation, sepsis, and multi-organ failure, often with fatal consequences.

The Immune System's Role

A Strongyloides infection may appear dormant until the host's immune system begins to mount a response. Ironically, this is often when the most severe complications arise. The parasite employs sophisticated mechanisms to evade immune attack, including altering its surface proteins, suppressing inflammatory responses, and redirecting host defenses. This ability to manipulate the immune system allows it to proliferate rapidly under the radar, causing significant harm to its host.

Protozoa

"Toxoplasmosis infects rats, then cats, then humans who make cat videos.

AI trains achieve superhuman intelligence training on Internet cat videos, thus making toxoplasmosis the true arbiter of our destiny."

- Elon Musk

While this quote from Elon Musk may seem humorous, it underscores the unsettling possibility of parasitic manipulation in humans, drawing attention to **Toxoplasma gondii**, a protozoan with an alarming influence on behavior and biology.

Behavioral Manipulation

T. gondii has been widely studied for its ability to alter rodent behavior. Infected rats exhibit reduced fear of cats, even being drawn to the smell of cat urine. This counterintuitive behavior makes the rodent more likely to be preyed upon, ensuring the parasite completes its life cycle in the cat's intestines, its definitive host.

What makes T. gondii fascinating—and concerning—is the hypothesis that it may similarly manipulate human behavior. Some studies suggest correlations between T. gondii infections and increased risk-taking, impulsivity, or even altered personality traits. Though the exact mechanisms remain elusive, one possibility is that the parasite alters neurotransmitter pathways, particularly those involving dopamine.

A Hidden Epidemic

T. gondii infections are alarmingly common, affecting an estimated **30-50% of the global population**. Most infections are asymptomatic in healthy individuals, but in immunocompromised people, such as those with HIV/AIDS or undergoing immunosuppressive therapy, the parasite can cause severe complications, including encephalitis and vision loss. Even in ostensibly healthy individuals, there's growing evidence linking latent T. gondii infection to psychiatric disorders like schizophrenia and bipolar disorder.

Some evidence points to the fact that we are acquiring this parasite not just from cats but from our produce in stores!

T. gondii and the Immune System

T. gondii's ability to invade host cells and hijack cellular machinery is key to its success. Once inside, it creates a protective structure known as the parasitophorous vacuole, which shields it from the immune system. This clever evasion strategy allows T. gondii to persist chronically in tissues, particularly in the brain, where it may subtly influence host behavior.

However, the parasite doesn't always go unnoticed. When the immune system detects T. gondii, it often triggers a robust response, which can result in inflammation and tissue damage. This inflammatory process may contribute to some of the long-term health effects associated with chronic infection.

Parasites - Deep Dive on Protozoa

The idea that parasites influence behavior extends far beyond rodents and toxoplasmosis. Emerging evidence hints that **protozoa** and **helminths** might alter human behaviors, affecting aspects as profound as voting patterns, sexual preferences, or even susceptibility to authoritarianism.

Parasites and Sexual Preferences

"In a controlled study, 67.5% of 200 homosexual men, but only 16% of 100 heterosexual men, were found to be infected with intestinal parasites."

*- **PMID:** 7437971*

This study links intestinal protozoa such as *Giardia* and *Entamoeba* to homosexuality. Although this correlation is intriguing, it remains uncertain whether the parasites directly manipulate sexual orientation or if other factors—such as environmental or lifestyle differences—play a role.

Interestingly, another study examined how *Toxoplasma gondii* might influence sexual behavior:

"Generally, infected subjects expressed relatively high attraction to nonconventional sexual practices, particularly BDSM-related activities. However, they reported engaging in these behaviors less frequently than the Toxoplasma-free subjects."

*- **PMID:** 29259726*

These findings suggest that *T. gondii*, unlike *Giardia* or *Entamoeba*, may not correlate with sexual orientation but rather with a preference for specific sexual behaviors. This makes sense, given *T. gondii*'s ability to affect the brain and hormonal systems, unlike the gut-dwelling *Giardia* and *Entamoeba*.

Mechanisms of Behavioral Manipulation

T. gondii appears to alter host behavior through hormonal modulation. For instance, studies in rodents show that the parasite increases testosterone levels by infecting immune-privileged sites like the brain and testes:

> "An alternative nontropic model suggests that the parasite manipulates communication between the brain and gonadal hormones. Toxoplasma invades rat testes upon infection, leading to a heavy cyst burden in the epididymis and ejaculates... The infection upregulates testosterone synthesis within Leydig cells of the testes."

- *doi.org/10.1371/journal.ppat.1004935*

This hormonal surge may enhance pheromone synthesis, attracting mates, and pushing the host toward riskier behaviors, including sexual ones. Whether similar mechanisms apply to humans remains an open question.

In contrast, *Giardia* and *Entamoeba* appear to correlate with homosexuality potentially due to their gut colonization patterns. If they are transmitted through the oral-fecal route, as suspected, the parasites might encourage anal sex to enhance their spread. The exact mechanisms remain speculative and warrant further research.

Parasites and Authoritarianism

Another provocative link between parasites and behavior involves decision-making in the context of governance:

"According to a 'parasite stress' hypothesis, authoritarian governments are more likely to emerge in regions characterized by a high prevalence of disease-causing pathogens."

- PMID: 23658718

This hypothesis suggests that parasite prevalence fosters fear-based decision-making, increasing susceptibility to authoritarian ideologies. The immune burden and chronic stress associated with infections might make populations more inclined to seek control and stability, even at the cost of personal freedoms.

Concluding Parasites

While the mentioned theories may seem far-fetched, they highlight the profound influence that parasites could exert on human behavior. The correlations between infection and behavioral changes are compelling, though much of the research remains theoretical. What is clear, however, is the need for better health practices to fortify the immune system and reduce vulnerability to opportunistic infections.

By improving individual and societal health, we can mitigate the subtle yet potentially far-reaching influence of parasitic infections on human decisions and behaviors.

Xenobiotics (Heavy Metals & Chemicals)

For the sake of efficiency, chemicals that exist within our systems are going to be discussed under 'Environmental Pollutants,' as that is the primary source of absorption.

Heavy Metals

Prior to this section of the book, we discussed the roles of minerals in the body. Heavy metals are the primary and direct disruptors of these minerals, alongside plant toxins, microbial interference, trauma, and health issues that contribute to mineral depletion.

Here is a basic overview of the more central toxic heavy metals in society today that **affect our sex hormones:**

Mercury

Mercury disrupts the hypothalamic-pituitary-gonadal (HPG) axis, which controls the production of sex hormones. It can reduce **testosterone** in men and affect **estrogen** and **progesterone** levels in women. Mercury binds to selenium and disrupts enzymes involved in hormone production, leading to fertility issues, irregular menstrual cycles, and lowered libido.

Mercury is personal for me, as it is for many in my generation. Vaccine preservatives like thimerosal, which contains mercury, were commonly used for children during my time. Thimerosal was added to vaccines to prevent bacterial or fungal contamination during storage. On top of that, my mother had "silver fillings," which are partly composed of mercury, which can slowly leach out, moving into vulnerable areas such as the brain and placenta. I've been working on removing the mercury from my body for several years, and I've noticed an unexpected yet gradual reduction in my ADD symptoms.

This connection is something I've been exploring more deeply, as it's become clear that heavy metals can disrupt neurological function and contribute to symptoms of ADD/ADHD and other cognitive issues.

Lead

Lead exposure can lead to reduced **testosterone** in men, lower sperm counts, and fertility issues. In women, lead can disrupt **estrogen** levels, causing menstrual irregularities and impaired fertility. Lead can interfere with the hypothalamic-pituitary axis and damage reproductive organs. It affects follicle-stimulating hormone (FSH) and luteinizing hormone (LH), which are crucial for reproductive health.

Lead is an interesting one. Although I don't have extensive client cases involving lead yet—since I've only recently started incorporating HTMA (Hair Tissue Mineral Analysis) into my practice—what I've found in research paints a compelling picture. Lead has strong correlations with neurological conditions like autism, heightened aggression, and even violent tendencies. Over time, I suspect I'll gather enough data to hypothesize a connection between lead exposure and certain behavioral patterns, like sexual sadism. While this is speculative at the moment, the parallels in how lead influences brain function and behavioral dysregulation are intriguing.

One thing that often surprises people is how lead can sneak into everyday essentials, like salt—even sea salt. It's similar to chocolate in that way; both are susceptible to heavy metal contamination. Ever notice how chocolate brands don't advertise "100% free from heavy metals"? It's not an accident—it reflects how widespread and persistent these contaminants can be in our food systems. For salt, finding options entirely free of lead can feel like an uphill battle, but it's worth the effort to reduce cumulative exposure.

Cadmium

Cadmium has **estrogen**-like effects, often termed xenoestrogenic. It can **mimic estrogen**, leading to hormonal imbalances in both men and women. This can cause issues like breast tissue growth in men (gynecomastia) and hormonal cancers in women (**breast cancer risk**). Cadmium interacts with **estrogen receptors**, disrupting normal hormonal signaling. It can also impair **testosterone synthesis in men**, reducing sperm quality and leading to infertility.

One of my clients reached out to me concerned about issues with copper utilization and low iron levels identified in their bloodwork. They had a history of diabetes mellitus 1.5 and liver complications linked to low ceruloplasmin. Based on how they described their situation, I suspected environmental factors—particularly heavy metals from their career. They had worked in an auto body shop for over 20 years, which immediately made me consider the potential impact of cadmium exposure on their liver.

To investigate further, they opted for a hair tissue mineral analysis (HTMA) through my services. The results confirmed elevated cadmium levels.

Cadmium is known to antagonize zinc in the liver, creating imbalances in copper metabolism that can reduce ceruloplasmin production. Low ceruloplasmin, in turn, can disrupt iron availability in the blood. Additionally, with a compromised immune system—commonly seen in diabetes—opportunistic microbes might exploit this type of environment, potentially targeting iron reserves.

As of this writing, my client has started to see positive changes in their insulin levels through targeted dietary adjustments. The next step in their health journey will involve strategies to displace cadmium from its receptor sites and restore balance.

Aluminum

Aluminum can accumulate in the **reproductive organs** and disrupt the **endocrine system**, leading to imbalances in **testosterone** and **estrogen**. There are links between **aluminum exposure** and reduced sperm quality in men. Aluminum interferes with estrogen receptors and alters hormone synthesis, potentially leading to infertility and **hormonal cancers**.

Aluminum is an often overlooked yet insidious agent present in many vaccines, particularly in the form of adjuvants. Its primary purpose isn't to benefit the body but rather to provoke a heightened immune response by introducing toxicity into the bloodstream. This process can teach the immune system to react more aggressively in the future, sometimes targeting harmless substances in a hyper-reactive manner.

While aluminum is commonly found in food, such as in salt or certain processed products, the digestive system is generally equipped to process and eliminate it, though it remains toxic. The real concern arises when aluminum is injected directly into the body. Bypassing the digestive system, it enters the bloodstream and can accumulate in critical organs like the brain, bones, and lymph nodes. This is a significant issue, as the kidneys may not always be able to clear all of it, leading to potential long-term health consequences

Arsenic

Arsenic can disrupt reproductive hormones, particularly by affecting **estrogen metabolism**. Prolonged exposure can lead to irregular menstrual cycles, decreased fertility, and pregnancy complications. Arsenic can alter the functioning of the HPG axis and impair estrogen metabolism in the liver, leading to **estrogen dominance** or deficiency.

Hexavalent chromium

Hexavalent chromium is associated with reproductive toxicity, affecting **testosterone** levels and sperm quality in men. In women, it may affect ovarian function and hormonal regulation, leading to infertility. Chromium can induce oxidative stress in reproductive tissues and interfere with the synthesis of sex hormones like **testosterone** and **estrogen**.

Nickel

High nickel exposure can impact **sex hormone regulation** by affecting the levels of **testosterone** and **estrogen**. It has been linked to reduced fertility and hormonal disruptions in both men and women. Nickel interferes with enzymes involved in **steroid hormone production** and may act as an **endocrine disruptor** by binding to **hormone receptors**.

Concluding Heavy Metals

Beyond what these heavy metals do on their own when we are exposed to them, they also contribute to significant mineral imbalances that generally disrupt the entire ionomic system. Minerals like **zinc**, **copper**, **calcium**, and **magnesium** can be displaced by heavy metals. This imbalance can lead to significant disruptions in **endocrine functioning**, especially when it comes to the **zinc to copper ratio**.

Based on my personal experiences with my health and my work with others, I believe that heavy metals, such as mercury, can trap individuals in a prolonged state of **fight-or-flight**, especially following a traumatic event. However, this isn't well charted by scientific literature and needs more research; it is merely my suspicion.

Many of these heavy metals can be found in our tap water, and fast food restaurants have a staggering amount of heavy metals as well. If you're a big fan of potatoes, you may want to learn about the effects of cadmium.

Environmental & Lifestyle Pollutants

Electromagnetic Frequencies (EMF)

EMF (electromagnetic fields) refers to all types of electromagnetic radiation, ranging from low-frequency waves (like those from power lines) to high-frequency waves (like gamma rays). This spectrum includes radio waves (RF), microwaves, Wi-Fi, infrared, visible light, X-rays, and gamma rays.

Numerous studies suggest that Non-native EMFs (nnEMFs), which are man-made EMFs, may disrupt endocrine function, although these findings are not often emphasized in the mainstream.

For instance:

"Cell phone RF exposure induced significant hormonal and structural changes in adrenal gland and brain tissues. Therefore, the public should be aware and limit their exposure as much as possible."

- **PMID:** 30627371

> *"From this study, it is concluded that Wi-Fi radiation causes invisible damaging effects by increasing the levels of salivary cortisol, necessitating vigorous measures to safeguard ourselves from these radiations."*

- 10.9734/jpri/2021/v33i41B32362

> *"These results indicate that a 900 MHz EMF emitted by cellular phones, especially with long-term exposure, increased serum cortisol and T4 levels while decreasing T3 levels, suggesting it can disrupt the endocrine system."*

- *January 2009 Bulletin of the Veterinary Institute in Pulawy 53(2):233-236*

While I'm by no means an expert in this area, I can speak from personal experience—both from watching my mother's health deteriorate when exposed to nnEMFs and from experiencing disrupted sleep with Wi-Fi on—that something is indeed amiss. RFK Jr. has dedicated significant work to this issue, documenting many case accounts linking cell phone use to cancer.

Air and Water Pollution

This is fairly common knowledge, but I recognize that many readers may be familiar with some areas and not others.

When it comes to water pollution, our water systems are regulated by the government. Depending on where someone lives, tap water—which many drink and shower with—often contains disinfecting agents to keep microbes at bay. While we've been led to believe this is beneficial, the consequence is that our skin absorbs these chemicals. Commonly found in waterways are fluoride and chlorine, but others include atrazine, glyphosate, antibiotics, hormones, pain relievers, nitrites and nitrates, trihalomethanes, haloacetic acids, many of the heavy metals mentioned earlier, and more.

The takeaway here is to filter your water.

With air pollution, we face:

Particles with a diameter of 10 micrometers or less, including dust, pollen, mold, and ash. Finer particles, 2.5 micrometers or smaller, can penetrate deep into the lungs and even enter the bloodstream. These come from combustion sources like cars, power plants, and industrial processes.

While there's a more detailed discussion needed on this subject, it somewhat detracts from our focus on endocrine and hormone health. Just bear in mind that air pollution presents many known problems, as well as issues we haven't yet been made aware of.

Clothing, Household Wares, Personal Care Products, and so on...

Our society is increasingly saturated with chemicals that permeate everyday life. From the clothing we wear to the products we use in our homes and on our bodies, exposure to toxins is nearly constant. This unrelenting exposure can have significant health implications, especially for those most vulnerable, such as pregnant women and children. For example, women using makeup containing phthalates during pregnancy may unknowingly expose their developing child to chemicals that can disrupt endocrine function, potentially leading to long-term health issues.

— Rudel, R. A., et al. (2011). "Phthalates and endocrine disruption in women: A review of the literature." Environmental Health Perspectives, 119(2), 305-313.

Synthetic Fabrics (Polyester, Nylon, Acrylic, etc.):

Synthetic fabrics such as polyester, nylon, and acrylic are commonly treated with chemicals like flame retardants, dyes, and formaldehyde. These chemicals, especially when heated or in contact with the skin, can release toxic gases into the environment. Studies have shown that flame retardants, for example, are linked to hormonal disruption and neurodevelopmental delays.

— Alcock, R. E., et al. (2010). "Flame retardants and health risks." Environmental Health Perspectives, 118(3), A126–A127.

— Stapleton, H. M., et al. (2011). "Flame retardants and their neurotoxic effects." Environmental Science & Technology, 45(1), 56-67.

Household Wares:

Many household items pose similar risks, particularly those made from materials like Teflon, aluminum, and plastics. Teflon-coated cookware, for instance, can release perfluorooctanoic acid (PFOA) when overheated, a chemical associated with various health problems including endocrine disruption. BPA and phthalates, commonly found in plastics, have been shown to interfere with hormonal regulation and are linked to conditions like obesity, diabetes, and developmental abnormalities. Copper toxicity can also arise from unlined copper cookware, while lead and cadmium, which may be present in certain glassware and enamel-coated cookware, are well-known for their neurotoxic and endocrine-disrupting effects.

— Gauthier, R. T., et al. (2008). "PFOA exposure and effects." Environmental Health Perspectives, 116(4), 444-451.

— Diamanti-Kandarakis, E., et al. (2009). "Endocrine-disrupting chemicals: An endocrine society scientific statement." Endocrine Reviews, 30(4), 293–342.

— Lidsky, T. I., & Schneider, J. S. (2003). "Lead neurotoxicity in children: Basic mechanisms and clinical correlates." Brain, 126(1), 5–19.

Personal Care Products:

The personal care industry is another significant source of harmful chemicals. Ingredients like parabens, phthalates, formaldehyde, and triclosan are commonly found in everyday products such as shampoos, lotions, and nail polish. Parabens, in particular, are widely recognized as endocrine disruptors that can mimic estrogen in the body, potentially contributing to breast cancer and reproductive issues. Phthalates, found in fragrances and plastics, have been associated with increased risks of birth defects and hormonal imbalances.

— Darbre, P. D., & Harvey, P. W. (2008). "Endocrine disrupting chemicals and breast cancer risk." Environmental Health Perspectives, 116(2), A41–A45.

— Swan, S. H., et al. (2005). "Phthalate exposure and the risk of developmental defects." Environmental Health Perspectives, 113(4), 483–488.

These examples highlight just a fraction of the chemicals that individuals are exposed to on a daily basis, many of which may contribute to chronic health issues, particularly affecting the endocrine system and reproductive health.

Conclusion of Xenobiotics

Our food, environment, household items, and even the people around us present countless exposure points to bodily toxins, which can feel overwhelming. Yet, there is always a path forward—steps we can take toward better health and minimizing the factors that threaten it from every angle.

Polarity Basics: Communication

Structure of Communication

For a basic overview, men—excluding the influence of the internet and telecommunications—are naturally inclined toward more physical communication and body language, reserving verbal communication for efficiency and necessity. Women, on the other hand, tend to focus more energy on verbal communication while also maintaining a notable degree of physical communication and body language.

Women

One of the most emphasized operative models for polarity dynamics in relationships is how women communicate. This is often termed *feminine communication (FC)*.

Generally, women are more collaborative and affiliative. They often converse to nurture and develop relationships. When experiencing a positive or negative stimulus, women tend to express how they feel rather than what they think. This emotional expression often comes across as a cry for help, which can hormonally drive men to respond and assist.

At its core, feminine communication isn't about being indirect to manipulate or orient a partner into action—it's about raw expression, free from direct judgment.

<u>Example</u>: A man accidentally steps on her foot. She exclaims, "Ow!" reacting to the pain without assigning blame. If the man is a good man, he'll immediately apologize, saying, "Oh wow, I'm sorry, I didn't see your foot there." If he's less considerate, he might respond, "You should watch where you're standing." Many women today might justify using this moment to strike back, but a flower is a flower— not a cactus with a bloom on top, as mentioned in the analogy at the beginning of this book. In her mastery of FC, she would simply express her hurt without engaging in a lesson-teaching response. As mentioned above, some men may not.

What often happens in these scenarios is that another man, noticing the rude response, might step in to correct the situation, fulfilling the role of protector. Women are intended to have protectors— other men around to compensate for situations where masculinity is required.

However, in today's highly individualistic world, women are often called upon to embody masculinity in scenarios where it's needed. A woman who has mastered FC and relationships is incredibly powerful in her own way, a fact that is often underestimated in modern society. I do also wish to disclaim that some scenarios can call for the woman to kick the masculine into gear for her own survival.

Men

When communicating with men, it's generally best to prioritize time efficiency. Every word a man speaks should be direct and purposeful. Ideally, he avoids unnecessary verbiage and keeps his communication concise and to the point. At a higher level, he anticipates what others will say and cuts straight to the solution.

While women can also excel in sharp, targeted communication, men are naturally inclined to speak less and lean more in physical communication than in verbal. They typically avoid adding fluff to their sentences unless the situation calls for it—such as when speaking with children or individuals with Down Syndrome.

Men's brains seem to process female voices differently than they do masculine or gender-ambiguous ones, engaging regions that reflect a more emotional and melodic interpretation. Research reveals that hearing a female voice activates the right anterior superior temporal gyrus (STG), a brain region associated with music and complex auditory processing. By contrast, male voices engage the precuneus, a region tied to mental imagery and spatial cognition.

"The results support the hypothesis that the perception of female voices activates human voice-selective regions in the right anterior superior temporal gyrus (STG) of the male brain. Contrasting the male brain's response to perceiving all male voices versus all female voices showed activation in the precuneus."

- https://doi.org/10.1016/j.neuroimage.2005.04.023

This distinction suggests that male voices are processed more pragmatically, focusing on spatial and contextual elements, while female voices elicit a response akin to experiencing music—rich, emotional, and resonant—showcasing the nuanced ways the brain interprets auditory stimuli based on gender.

Examples of man vs. woman with basic communication

Let me set the stage: communication styles between men and women are inherently different, and these differences are often misunderstood.

Woman (big smile): "It's so beautiful out today! I can't wait to go to the beach!" Based on her personality, she might extend this to, "It's so beautiful out today! The flowers, the gentle breeze—Oh! That puppy!"

Man (normal smile): "Nice day out. Let's go to the beach."

Now, don't get lost in the extroversion vs. introversion debate here. While certain cognitive types may stray from polarized communication, it's still possible to learn a style that aligns with their natural mindset.

The key difference between feminine and masculine communication lies in focus:

Men are solution-oriented, operating primarily from a thought process rooted in judgment and logic.

Women, on the other hand, are generally focused on love and emotion. Ideally, their communication carries an unassuming, uplifting, and even musical quality.

Both men and women are capable of communicating in both ways and should develop both skills. However, they naturally lean toward one style more than the other. The issue arises when men consistently adopt feminine communication patterns, or women default to masculine ones.

It's crucial for a woman to avoid dwelling in judgment. Only when absolutely necessary should she bring in that "masculine iron fist" of logic. Men, by contrast, should stay focused on identifying root causes, making sound judgments, and offering actionable solutions, rarely veering into emotional fluff or overly casual conversation.

Of course, not every scenario fits neatly into these dynamics, and context matters. Generally, though, men should embody a stoic, grounded energy, while women should express a freer, more flowing energy. Women thrive when focusing on inspiration, while men thrive when driving forward with solid solutions.

The Permissive Language Model & Feminine Communication (FC)

"May I speak?" "Please may I step away?" "I wish to share my feelings..."

I call this the 'permissive language model,' which is often pushed by some of the most popular polarity coaches as 'feminine communication.' This model, I believe, is overly utilized and can lead a woman to become a nuisance to the masculine ROI-focused men they're romantically engaged with. Though it's not to say that it is bad or useless. I am not one to throw the baby out with the bath water.

Masculine men aren't looking to dilly-dally with communication. They want it to be concise and efficient. A man who has to give her permission to speak with every other sentence she utters is wasting his time. Yes, it can be effective in particular moments when the woman seeks to be more submissive and receptive to his authority, as it directly influences both her and his psyche. However, it often crosses boundaries and can become excessive.

What some of the polarity coaches are doing with their style is reproducing a dominant and submissive dynamic offered in the world of kink, but reframing it to fit a traditional relationship/marriage. Hence, why these coaches have become so popular—because many men and women find this style of romantic interaction to be very attractive and pervasive to their nervous system. This way of operating is often driven by voids from what someone lacked during upbringing.

People can do what they want; I'm not here to police anyone's choices of what they're doing behind closed doors, but I do want to stand for what 'polarity' really is and separate models like the one mentioned above into a subcategory, rather than it being seen as the main category.

More on Feminine Communication

Feminine communication is in itself more permissive in nature, however, the one outlier is that men have feminine aspects within themselves, and women have masculine aspects. **Efficient language between the sexes is blended**.

Under a permissive model, a girl after a successful date could say in a text message (or not at all, because some coaches push no initiation socially at all):

"May I express how I feel?"

The guy could see it right away, or not. Either way, it's inconvenient for both parties. When a woman is not going the permissive route and just immediately expresses how she feels in a feminine way, it can be fairly successful.

Example:

"I really had a good time last night, I am SO grateful for you setting it all up and buying me dinner. I hope to see you again!"

This way, she is **initiating with vulnerability**. Depending on the man, he may have first exclaimed how he felt, but the woman should generally be more expressive and free flow with how she feels before the man does. In the scenario where he expresses first (which is okay because some personality types/archetypes are just this way no matter how masculine they become), she can still express nearly the same sentence quoted above.

Situational Examples

The First Approach - Male View

Contrary to popular belief, this phase should come with as little verbal communication as possible **in-person**. A good portion of a man's initial perception of a woman is influenced by her posture, gait, and how she interacts with those around her. These factors should guide his first approach instinctively, without a cascade of thoughts or worries. If he is genuinely in a masculine frame of mind, he should be able to approach with natural confidence.

This was one of the first benefits I noticed after my beard went red in several areas back when I became much more masculine. I went from contemplating strategies, or waiting for moments to approach a woman I liked, to instantly going up to them and keeping it very simple:

Me: "Wow, the way you engage the world around you pulled me in (it's good for a man to tell a woman that they have some legitimate reason for approaching that isn't giving off the vibe that the man is "thirsty"), are you married (this tells her that he has a stopping point and sense of what's right and wrong)?

Her: [some basic response of yes or no with a 'thank you.']

Me: [I will generally say what we are doing next and immediately start taking command from this point to get her to psychologically follow suit and go with my lead.]

Typically, this approach results in exchanging numbers most of the time, provided the individuals are not in happy relationships and find the man attractive. It's important to note that I developed all of this through pure instinct and soon realized that it doesn't function as effectively when I'm not in a masculine frame of mind. In my first year of operating this way, I wasn't always fully in that masculine frame of mind and occasionally lost some of my vibrant masculinity. Nevertheless, this method of communicating with women can still be effective. However, it's much more apparent to women when a man is in the right mindset, as both parties can feel that hormonal connection.

This frame of mind is a core aspect of the 'emanating masculine.'

To articulate this fully, a man who leans into a feminine mindset may find himself preoccupied with what she might say or do. He might spend excessive time waiting for her to appear more approachable, which can be seen as masculine depending on the context. However, one could argue that the most masculine men will confidently approach even in a crowd of thousands. This man may also be ready with half-truths, focused on seeking a quick fix while knowing she isn't "the one." Ultimately, he is likely to lack a stoic, calm, and strong presence. A fearless man is the kind of energy she should truly feel.

The First Approach - Female View

The same can apply to women, but their journey is different in that an average woman can pull in the sexual interest of a large number of men regardless of being 'radiantly feminine.' Due to society being fairly contorted, where the father and any other men around aren't there to ensure she finds an ideal mate, she often has to masculinize her behavior to some extent to establish boundaries that deter boys from seeking a quick "fix".

This often comes as a consequence for her, because the more masculine she becomes when doing this, the more (oftentimes fatherless) boys she attracts, and the more masculine men she pushes away. This goes back to the cactus analogy mentioned earlier.

The most profound wisdom I can share with women today is to be vulnerable and observe what a man does with the power given to him through her vulnerability. **A true test of his character is to give him the opportunity to reveal who he really is**.

Many don't fully understand how this dynamic works, but women are the initiators of love through vulnerability. Men may approach first, but they are not the activators. In some cases, a woman may not even realize her feminine energy is drawing a man in—and that's perfectly fine, as she is meant to be a passive attractor. However, she should ideally find a way to learn about the man and develop respect for him. When women make men chase them or treat them like jesters, it's inefficient and reflects a large ego rooted in a masculine mindset. Women who are feminine and receptive will naturally be curious about others and want to know all about the man in front of them.

When a woman is leaning more feminine during a date, her guard isn't up and she is asking questions in no way outside of sheer interest. It should feel entirely innocent to him, coming from her heart on a genuine level. I don't recommend faking this, and instead just being that kind of woman. If she isn't significantly affected by ADD/ADHD (I have always had ADD and have only recently learned to center myself and truly listen to others), she will typically be an attentive listener. This attentiveness is often reciprocated by him if he is a genuinely decent masculine man.

When she embodies a more masculine energy on a date, she may present herself well and soften her words to appear feminine; however, there is often an underlying mission to analyze and silently assess the man. Depending on her personality or archetype, she might be very direct and upfront about this. In my experience, women who are in fight-or-flight mode or who have PCOS may exhibit this behavior due to the androgenic hormonal influences they often experience.

Daily Routine - Feminine Expression & Vulnerability

Once a relationship has settled into a routine, numerous communication challenges can arise, particularly for women. One common scenario is when a man neglects a responsibility he committed to, and it remains undone. Many women, in response, quickly jump to judgment and take on either a motherly or fatherly approach to handling the situation, which often leads to long-term dissatisfaction.

Men need to experience the consequences of their own mistakes. One of the most motivating consequences for a masculine man to take action is seeing the woman he deeply cares about express genuine overwhelm. If she avoids judgment—let's say she's making dinner in the kitchen while he's unwinding on the couch after a long day—she only needs to express how she feels. Many women I've coached struggle with this, often mixing up her judgment of him with her own feelings. However, a woman who releases blame and judgment can simply communicate her emotional state in the moment. This opens the door for the man to respond instinctively, wanting to help without hesitation.

Now, if she falls into a long-term pattern of subtly leading him by taking the trash to the door and asking him sweetly for help, she is slipping into a mothering role. If she directly tells him it's his responsibility to take out the trash, she is assuming a fatherly role. Neither option is beneficial. Both scenarios make her feel as though she is in control and more responsible than he is within the household. This dynamic, where roles become inverted, undermines the natural balance needed for a healthy, romantic relationship. It disrupts the foundation for long-term partnership and procreation.

Daily Routine - Masculine Stoicism

A significant issue for men is how they communicate with women, especially when it comes to complaining after a hard day at work. A man's wife or girlfriend isn't meant to be his mother, even though this may be a difficult truth for some men to accept. It's one thing to be genuinely hurt by a serious challenge, and quite another to come home complaining about a coworker who used the wrong sandpaper on a project. Masculine men, when faced with danger—like narrowly dodging a car—don't react with fear or shock by saying,

"Oh my gosh! I almost died!" They just calmly acknowledge, "...cool, I dodged that car." In fact, if they're truly battle-tested, they wouldn't even flinch and would continue on with their work without missing a beat.

However, when a man is truly shaken by a significant loss or challenge, his partner needs to be there for him. She must show empathy without judgment. Even the greatest men can falter, as nothing in this world is immune to the chaos life can bring. No man of value wants a woman who abandons ship at the first sign of trouble because her doing so increases the risk of failure. For men reading this, it's okay to share your vulnerabilities and deep struggles with a woman when it's something significant. While traditional relationship advice might suggest women will be repulsed by a man who shows emotional weakness, this advice often comes from women who are wounded themselves, likely due to poor father relationships.

Ultimately, men need a woman who can stand strong, even in the face of his deepest struggles or if he is gone. This resilience in a woman is not only essential for emotional health, but it's also a critical survival strategy.

Handling Discourse

As a disclaimer, a polarized relationship in which both partners are actively engaged in the dynamics of discourse versus a situation where only one person is committed to this approach results in dramatically different outcomes. In general, I don't advise following all of the principles of polarity and traditional relationships when one person is the only one actively pursuing it within the relationship.

Ideally, an optimal polarized relationship should have minimal, if any, arguments. This is the essence of polarity, where the flow between the sexes is so aligned that harmony is achieved. I can say from experience that I've met couples married for 50+ years who have never argued, and I myself have experienced polarized dynamics with women where turbulence is almost nonexistent. This is largely because the feminine woman, when she places her trust in a man, doesn't assume or worry about him. When she boards his ship, she lets go of any future concerns about the journey—therefore, no complications arise.

You might think this sounds idealistic, but it is very much possible, as long as the man is upfront about everything from the start.

Example:

Man: "Hey beautiful, this is my ship, this is what my ship is made of, this is what kind of man I am. This is where I lack, this is where I'm great, and this is what you can expect on the journey forward with me. These are my expectations of you, and I hold myself to this standard. These are my beliefs, and I want kids at this point, etc."

The point is, women need to stop expecting a specific kind of 'game' from men and instead seek a man who establishes the rules of engagement from the beginning. It will save them—and the world—a lot of trouble.

Polarity Basics: Core Structure

There are fundamental systems of polarity that are essential to understand, as they provide clarity on a topic that, while ancient, is gaining newfound attention and relevance in today's society.

Competency & Vulnerability

As explained in the Defining Polarity chapter, vulnerability and competency are key components of masculinity and femininity in relationships. The father is meant to bring a skill set of competency for survival, while the mother imparts the ability to be vulnerable, a crucial trait for emotional and relational survival. But how does this manifest in a polarized relationship?

Both men and women have the capacity for both competency and vulnerability, but competency is primarily a masculine trait, while vulnerability is inherently feminine. For the relationship to thrive, the man must recognize that the woman has a certain level of competency while maintaining her core feminine strength— vulnerability. Likewise, she must see that he has the ability to be vulnerable, to truly listen to her, and to demonstrate the competence necessary to guide and raise children.

Vulnerability

From a woman's vulnerability comes her ability to access boundless love and uplift those around her. When a woman is in a state of needing a man, her vulnerability naturally emerges, creating space for her to tap into her most powerful qualities as a mother and someone with profound spiritual gifts. I won't dive into the specifics of the spiritual capacities that women often seem to possess more than men, but in my experience, women who embrace vulnerability have greater access to this potential.

When she can direct her energy toward creativity, spiritual well-being, and nurturing children—while the man carries the weight of masculine responsibilities, which he is willing to do—her entire environment, from the home to the broader community, begins to thrive. Imagine the immense potential of humanity if women were able to fully embody their peak selves as a source of inspiration and creative force.

Vulnerability in the Relationship

When a woman chooses vulnerability in her communication, she doesn't present herself like a man to her partner, even during challenging moments. If she does choose vulnerability, he can then launch with enthusiasm for solving her problems. On the other hand, if she becomes overly defensive or falls into a more masculine role, the man may retreat into a passive feminine state, which can be detrimental to the relationship.

If a woman expects a man to submit with vulnerability to her, it signals that the relationship hasn't been properly established. The moment she agrees to be with him should also be the moment she fully trusts him and lets go of any doubts. While this may sound risky in today's world, it ultimately depends on the caliber of the man and her judgment in choosing him. A woman's vetting process is most effective when the man is introduced to her father. The father should be the one who assesses the man and assures her that his instinct aligns with her own intuition.

When a woman is at her most receptive, her vulnerability becomes a powerful tool that sharpens her intuition. While this might seem esoteric, I've witnessed it firsthand and felt the energy of such women—it's transformative. This is why it's so important for women to let go of control and entrust it to a good man. Doing so not only enhances his instinctual abilities but strengthens the dynamic between them.

Vulnerability in Men

If the reader remembers from the Defining Polarity chapter of the book, I articulate that men and women optimally embody a percentage of the opposite sex within them. When it comes to men and their ability to be vulnerable, this book itself is a great example of that. I've shared with the reader and others who have read it a very vulnerable section of my life, and plan to write another book with even more details of the story. Without utilizing vulnerability by sharing my story, I will have made a weaker argument for polarity, as people want to see both an intellectual argument with something that makes it real, like a story.

Vulnerability for a man can in a lot of ways be a form of competency. It is instead coming from the feminine side of his mind. Men also need to be receptive and vulnerable to men in their Brotherhood, as well as with the seniors that guide them. This is all tied to an optimal way of living for survival and life fulfillment.

Competency

Competency should be viewed as a man's toolkit—everything from how he provides for his family to how he strategizes to ensure their success, to how he navigates the dynamics of relationships, both with loved ones and the people who respect him within his community.

Without his competency to survive, there is no life to be lived on earth. Competency forms the foundation of everything that allows us to exist. This is why it is crucial for the man to lead the "how"—the mission here on earth—while she embodies the "why"—the purpose behind it all.

It is important to note that commonly feminine skill sets such as 'feminine communication' or dance are forms of competency. The man in the family is intended to guide the children in utilizing these skills to achieve a desired outcome.

Realism of Competency

Today, competency is more nuanced. Men and women can earn money in a variety of ways, many of which can feel inherently unnatural. However, when we come together as a society—a civilization—the dynamic shifts. Even Jesus, by traditional standards, was competent but poor before he was given wealth. Many women would still have chosen to procreate with him, given the chance, showing that the common internet advice suggesting women are solely attracted to power and money isn't entirely accurate. Yes, women are drawn to a man's power, particularly when he demonstrates a humble superiority over others, but this doesn't always equate to financial wealth. This concept will be explored further under the section 'Provision.'

Competency in the Relationship

For a family to thrive, a man must possess a level of competence and leadership that surpasses his partner's. Without this, a woman may struggle to surrender control and can end up questioning his abilities, particularly if she is operating from a place of survival. This is one reason I believe society should reconsider pushing girls to provide for themselves by 18. When women are forced into independence at an early age, they often develop more masculine traits, which can diminish their value in relationships. As women grow more competent and self-reliant, the pool of compatible men shrinks. At the same time, they may feel more internally fulfilled because they unconsciously step into a masculine role.

When a man has his own agency and takes charge of his life, he develops the competence needed to earn a woman's respect and admiration. This, in turn, allows her to express her femininity freely enough to inspire him.

It's a hard truth for men, but if they fail to prove they can protect and provide, the polarity won't align. A man cannot reach his greatest potential if he cannot provide for and protect a woman, just as she cannot reach hers without him. They need each other—especially in a survival context, where failing to make a kill means both could starve.

Competency in Women

Women must have competency, and for a man to respect her and really cherish her, he must see that she is capable of survival with or without him. However, she should not want to stay this way, and would widely be more focused on what I call 'female competency.'

The *Manifestor* man from the Developmental Archetypes section of the book is a man who often utilizes female competency to achieve outcomes in life, albeit in feminine ways. An example can be that he can have no problem asking for help when he needs it, he may also pray more often and hope that God will align for him the next steps, and he can choose to produce art or heal people to make a living. This is the same for women in that they can get from point A to point D just by leaning on others or manifesting energetically.

So while women can learn to wield an axe, drive a car, churn butter, wrestle cows, their most powerful potential and much more substantial resource lies within their female competency. A *babygirl* archetype, for example, can be more proficient in this area than a *Warrioress* who is more focused on **doing** rather than **being**.

Instinct & Intuition

[These definitions are just my personal view on instinct and intuition, and are not to be taken as absolute fact]

Both men and women possess both instinct and intuition, but generally, men tend to be more adept at instinct, while women excel more with intuition. This distinction holds true within a specific cultural and genetic context, as the natural roles and development of these traits are often shaped by those factors. For instance, a family with a strong spiritual lineage might produce men with heightened intuitive abilities, while a non-spiritual lineage could result in women being more in tune with their intuition. Of course, there will always be exceptions to this pattern, as every individual is unique.

Masculine Instinct

In times of crisis, masculine instinct often drives individuals to take swift, decisive actions aimed at ensuring safety, overcoming obstacles, or securing necessary resources. While this is a straightforward understanding of instinct, it can also be viewed as a **response to the physical world around us**.

When a man is in tune with peak masculine instinct, he may sense a threat to his child before it even fully manifests, prompting him to act with remarkable speed and precision. Masculine instinct, at its core, connects us to the tangible world and grounds us in our physical reality. It is this instinct that allows men to navigate challenges, maintain control, and exert mastery over the physical environment.

Feminine Intuition

Feminine intuition operates along the axis of receptivity, embodying a childlike purity that remains deeply connected to the ether, cosmos, spiritual realm, or whatever one chooses to call it. To some, it is believed that intuition in some ways can connect us to a kind of human consensus, assuming that we are all connected to some degree. As mentioned before, the feminine represents the child, and the masculine represents the adult.

> *"The reason I know this and you don't is because I'm younger and purer. So, I'm more in touch with cosmic forces."*

- Jonah from Sleepless in Seattle

At its core, feminine intuition can be seen as a **response to the subtle currents of energy and emotions that flow beneath the surface of everyday interactions**.

When a woman experiences heightened intuition, she might not always have the words to articulate what she senses, but there is a profound, almost visceral understanding in the moment. This feeling, though intangible, can provide her with the clarity needed to navigate situations with grace and insight. Some believe that intuition connects us to a higher realm, a deeper consensus, helping us tap into a wisdom that transcends logic and reason, guiding our decisions with an almost divine precision.

They both apply in both sexes

While intuition is often described as a feminine trait and instinct as masculine, it's important to recognize that both qualities exist in everyone for a reason. However, many people struggle to tap into their intuition and instead rely heavily on their immediate bodily experiences to guide their decisions.

In a polarized relationship, the beauty lies in the complementary roles that each partner plays. When a woman embraces her femininity and relinquishes control over real-world affairs to the man, she heightens her intuitive abilities. This, in turn, supports the man in his role, as her intuition can guide him in navigating the challenges and opportunities of the real world. By contrast, the man thrives in his masculine role, using her insights while leveraging his instinct and decisiveness to create stability and success.

The archetype of the *Manifestor* exemplifies this dynamic perfectly. As a man who embodies both feminine energy and a desire for masculine drive, the *Manifestor* uses his intuition to envision his dreams while channeling his masculine strength to make them a reality. The more grounded he becomes in his masculinity, the more effectively he can transform his visions into tangible success, blending these energies to create a life of purpose and achievement. However, for many *Manifestors* it is often that they very much struggle to achieve their dreams due to a lack of competency and overall capability.

Boundaries & Surrender

This topic often ignites heated debate, whether online or in real-life discussions involving psychology or human relationships. The reason it's so contentious is that I advocate for women, during courtship, to take an approach that may feel counterintuitive: easing or even temporarily lowering boundaries. Yes, you read that correctly—minimizing boundaries during courtship.

This doesn't mean abandoning safety or self-respect; rather, it's about fostering a natural dynamic between a man and a woman, unimpeded by rigid walls. By softening her boundaries, a woman creates a space where a man can authentically express his intentions, character, and ability to hold her vulnerability. This openness becomes a test of his masculinity—his capacity to protect, cherish, and honor her. Overly strict boundaries can mask a man's true nature, while openness enables her to fully experience and evaluate who he is.

Boundaries

Surrender and vulnerability aren't signs of weakness—they are among a woman's most powerful tools for discerning a suitor's worthiness. Surrender is an act of trust and release, while vulnerability is the courage to remain open, even at the risk of being hurt. By leaning into her intuition and observing how she feels, a woman can sense a man's energy and intentions.

A man's reaction to her openness reveals volumes about his character. Will he exploit her vulnerability, bulldozing her trust, or will he rise with integrity, exercising respect and self-control? On the first date, by granting him a measure of control—choosing where to go, for example—she gains insight into his nature. Does he demonstrate thoughtfulness and care, or does he act selfishly? Over time, her continued vulnerability allows her to assess his capacity for generosity, nobility, and commitment.

When a woman approaches courtship this way, surrender becomes a tool of discernment. It's not about passivity or recklessness but about creating space to evaluate whether a man is truly worthy of her trust and love.

Surrender

When a woman fully embraces her vulnerability and surrenders, she invites a man to step into his highest potential. This dynamic has the power to transform both partners. For instance, a man content with a steady, modest job might find himself inspired to reach for greater ambitions, perhaps starting a business or pursuing a dream he hadn't considered before. Her trust and surrender unlock his drive, while his responsibility and provision create a foundation for her to thrive.

In this dynamic, her surrender is not about dependence; it's about empowerment. Her freedom to radiate femininity becomes his responsibility, a challenge that a truly masculine man willingly accepts. His role as a provider and protector allows her to flourish, and her trust fuels his purpose. Together, they create a cycle of mutual growth and inspiration: her surrender motivates his ambition, and his ambition supports her radiance.

This balance of feminine trust and masculine responsibility is the essence of a powerful relationship. When both partners embrace their roles fully, they bring out the best in each other, forming a bond rooted in mutual respect, purpose, and growth.

The Tribe

It's essential to grasp that our biology has remained largely unchanged over thousands of years, even as evidence suggests humanity's existence stretches back hundreds of thousands of years. There's little reason to believe that our fundamental makeup has shifted significantly in that time. Yet, modern society often clings to the belief that progress and technology have made us biologically superior to our ancestors. In reality, the opposite is often true.

As explored in the Polarity Basics: Health section, our bodies are under constant assault from environmental toxins that compromise even the healthiest and most metabolically optimized among us. These challenges are compounded by inherited weaknesses passed down through generations, ensuring that almost no one escapes this modern paradigm unscathed.

The solution isn't to return entirely to primitive living but to integrate elements of the tribal model into modern life. By finding a balance—where civilization mirrors the natural world more closely—we can reclaim the level of health that allows us to embody the masculine and feminine ideals we're designed for. Health is the foundation of polarity: it empowers men to exude a commanding masculinity and enables women to radiate feminine vitality.

Ultimately, the tribal model serves as the blueprint for fostering the kind of relationships we aspire to in today's world. By incorporating its principles, we can create environments that nurture health, connection, and the essence of our shared humanity.

"It takes a tribe to raise a child"

The actual quote uses the word *village*, but my focus here is on how the past systems of living can serve as a blueprint for achieving optimal health and relationships today.

When a woman stays at home to raise children in isolation, her experience is often much harder and less fulfilling than it would be in a community setting. Many women feel unfulfilled when confined to the traditional role of a mother without the support or connection to others. In a tribal setting, a mother's role expands beyond her household. She can contribute to the tribe in meaningful ways, reinforcing its shared goals while still focusing on her children. At the same time, the tribe supports her in the difficult task of raising those children—offering guidance, help, and shared responsibility. While many mothers today manage alone, the results are rarely as seamless or enriching as they would be with collective involvement.

Although it may seem idealistic to imagine a world where communities gather, neighbors trust one another, and collective child-rearing thrives, it isn't out of reach. There is hope. Many good people share a desire to restore this sense of community, blending the best aspects of tribal living with the conveniences of modern life. While this book won't delve deeply into how to structure such a tribe or village, know that it's possible. The key lies in connection, cooperation, and a shared vision for healthier, more supportive lives.

Survival

In a tribal setting, life itself was very important, and each individual held immense value. With a much smaller population, the presence of any able-bodied man was far more significant to women than it is today. A capable hunter, especially one who could successfully hunt solo, was considered a remarkable asset. Women would feel profound gratitude not only for the men's safe return but also for the food they brought back. Living as hunter-gatherers optimized neurotransmitter balance, enabling people to handle stress better and avoid the mood swings that often strain relationships today. Harder lives forged stronger people, and with modern ease has come widespread weakness—impacting our relationships and our health.

During my time with Northwest Survival School under Travis Johnson in Spokane, WA, I confirmed what I had long suspected about life in the wild. The hunt was central, while foraging provided little sustenance. Early humans didn't immediately master agriculture; they migrated frequently, relying heavily on hunting to survive. Even Native American tribes a few hundred years ago lived similarly, moving often and dependent on hunting. Despite their primitive ways, they found happiness in their lives.

Today, there's an argument for leveraging modern advancements to maintain sovereignty and avoid exploitation, but our bodies remain poorly adapted to the modern lifestyle. The disconnect between our biology and contemporary life creates imbalance. While an anarchic return to a fully natural existence seems unlikely in our lifetimes, we can strive to live as naturally as possible, resisting systems that erode our health freedoms.

By embracing a more natural lifestyle and reclaiming primal health, we lay the groundwork for deeper, more polarized relationships. Hormonal and psychological balance is essential for this, and it thrives in a natural state. While perfection isn't required, the closer we are to optimal health, the more harmonious and fulfilling our relationships can become.

A radiant woman and emanating man in a tribal setting

The emanating man would likely be the chieftain, and the radiant woman would be something of a 'high seer' role likable to how the Avatar movie played out. I won't say that the characters in the movie resembled having peak character (the gender dynamics are a little modernized), but their roles in a tribal setting are good examples.

The radiant woman in a tribal setting would be the emotional and spiritual anchor, offering guidance and uplifting those in need. Her influence would not only foster individual growth but also strengthen the tribe's sense of purpose and connection to something higher. Her role is to serve as a bridge between the physical and spiritual realms to keep the tribe aligned with its collective goals. She would be an example of how vulnerability can be powerful, and how expression can be seen as necessary for survival.

The emanating man, leading by example on the hunt, would be the provider, protector, and balanced leader who earns both love and respect through his actions. His strength is complemented by his capacity for compassionate leadership, ensuring the tribe's cohesion and survival. This dynamic echoes the leadership styles of ancient warrior cultures, where strength, responsibility, and respect formed the foundation of effective leadership. The emanating man is called not only to command his people, but serve them.

Tribal Courtship

For many Native American, African, and Nordic tribes it was customary for a man seeking a woman to consummate with to earn the respect of her family by demonstrating competency in some capacity. Many tribes were very interdependent, and so to keep this cycle going in a positive motion, it was very important for the men who wanted to lead families to be capable of doing so.

Today, this is absolutely not the case for many cultures worldwide. Often, men can just up and create children by swiping right on an app. What took years of hard trials of survival of men in the past, now can be done in a day.

Moving away from this model has been incredibly destructive to society, and so with this passage of the book, I hope to call men and women alike to move toward these tribal examples. We should expect more men to approach the father, grandfather, brother, or any masculine figure she is close to—someone with competency and strong logic—with the confidence to earn their respect first.

The woman should focus on how he makes her **feel**, while the men should primarily rely on logical judgment to discern whether he is a good long-term fit for her. Their input shouldn't overwhelm her opinion, but it also shouldn't be disregarded.

The standard for marriage or commitment must be higher, or relationships will continue to deteriorate. The world has shifted too far toward 'yin energy,' enabling a culture of indulgence and fleeting pleasures. To restore balance, we must reintroduce more 'yang energy' to correct these imbalances.

Inspiration & Provision

For a man to feel the desire to provide for a woman, he needs to be inspired by her. His provision is what sustains their physical lives here on earth, while her inspiration elevates them both, bringing them closer to something divine. It's a balance that creates harmony between the practical and the transcendent.

As I once shared in my free polarity group online:

"Women bring men to heaven, and men bring women to earth."

Inspiration & Expression

Within the tribe, women have the power to inspire not only the men they share their lives with but anyone who witnesses their dance, song, or ability to spread love. Simply by offering a listening ear, a woman can encourage others to reach for more. The warmth she brings to others' hearts breathes life into them, sparking growth and connection.

When a woman has adequate provision and is in a parasympathetic, rest-and-digest state of mind, this ability to inspire is magnified. With his support, she can transform what he provides into so much more—multiplying its impact and, in turn, helping him become something greater than he was before.

How inspiration looks in reality

Women often wrestle with the idea of becoming a 'mother figure' to their lover, especially if they feel like they're playing the role of a cheerleader too often. However, this dynamic is highly context-dependent, shaped by the kind of inspiration she offers and when and how she chooses to express it.

A feminine woman who releases judgment and fully embraces the peace and comfort her masculine lover provides can surpass the typical relationship dynamic seen today. When a man comes home to her smiling warmly at the door, she's actively cheering him on— not through over-the-top efforts, but by being soft, comforting, and genuinely present. A woman can also sing to him, dance for him, or bring any additional moments of relief that help him disconnect from the harshness of his work life.

Another key factor is her vulnerability and openness to receiving him. When she allows herself to need him in this way, it gives the man a deeper sense of purpose within the home—not just through any potential children but through fulfilling the masculine role that completes and elevates their bond.

Provision

Provision brings stability and forms the foundation of a relationship. When a man provides, he's not just covering basic needs; he's creating a sense of security for her. This allows her to feel supported, enabling her to bring her own strengths forward and contribute to their shared life in a meaningful way.

In return for provision, she can take what he provides and multiply it. She's able to focus on what she brings—her warmth, creativity, and empathy—without the stress of survival. When she feels grounded and supported, she's free to improve life for both of them, creating something stronger than either could build alone.

How provision looks in reality

It's challenging for men today to provide, especially in countries with what I call an 'emasculating economy,' where people are burdened by heavy taxation. For this section, I'll focus specifically on the United States, where I have the knowledge and experience to provide for women with an average income.

The issue today is that women often have unusually high expectations regarding how much money a man should make, while men, even when in control of their finances, struggle with budgeting effectively.

This isn't intended as financial advice, but from my experience, I've managed on a modest budget for myself and a girlfriend. This can be done while maintaining optimal health and enjoying life. Now, I may have a history of living with very little, but it doesn't have to be that extreme. There are plenty of situations in which a man can budget enough to provide both himself and his woman with a roof over their heads, food to eat, water to drink, and enough cheap or free entertainment to truly enjoy life. It's about being smart, humble, and recognizing that happiness can be found in these simple, fulfilling experiences.

Provision is biodegradable

When provision was acquired among hunters and gatherers, it was generally biodegradable. Men crafted tools and other items from animal materials and resources found in the surrounding environment, but the primary form of provision was food. Men would share this with the tribe, and they likely wanted to do so. Studies have shown that men with higher testosterone often feel a strong desire to give to others. Men who are unwell, however, tend to become self-focused and lack the desire to lift others up. These are unfulfilled men.

This concept applies today as well. Families don't really need that much. As I write this book, I'm far from wealthy. I could have pursued a career in sales or entertainment and likely done very well, but my focus now is on this—bringing the truth forward during a pivotal time. I am happy, I love my life, and I'm confident that I can make a woman feel safe and comfortable without needing to earn a six or seven figure income.

Women want a man who can bring home the bacon, day in and day out. They desire a stable man who is more competent than they are and willing to do the hard work they would rather avoid. Many women also appreciate men who take big risks and reach for the heavens with a leap of faith. I'm definitely that man, but not all men are, and not all women need that risk-taker; nor does every man need to be that man.

We live in an interesting era today. People are eager to heal and reconnect with a more primal way of living. Old systems are fading, but even older systems are being resurrected. People are realizing that immense wealth doesn't necessarily bring happiness. It's the pursuit of living life together with family and tribe that brings fulfillment—where we go out, get the job done, survive, and return home to the camaraderie of song and dance around the fire.

Concluding Polarity Basics

Having a foundational understanding of polarity in relationships is an excellent first step toward enjoying a relationship free of arguments. When both partners operate in alignment with their natural roles, conflict becomes rare, and life feels significantly easier.

Polarity in relationships is so powerful that the pairing of a masculine man and a feminine woman can elevate not only themselves but also the tribe around them. It's truly one of the most optimal survival strategies, aligning with our nature and fostering deep happiness.

That said, it's crucial for the reader to understand that while this chapter provides a framework for embodying polarity within a relationship, it doesn't guarantee success for every unique situation.

For example, a woman might invest in one of the most expensive polarity coaching programs available to ignite, rekindle, or transform her relationship into something extraordinary. While such programs can offer significant benefits, there are potential pitfalls to be aware of. As I mentioned in the "ADD/ADHD & ASD" section of the book, certain neurodivergent pairings—such as an ADD/ADHD man and an ASD woman—can create foundational challenges in a relationship.

While there are ways to navigate such complexities, these solutions are nuanced and may not be fully addressed in this book. In such cases, I recommend investing in personalized guidance from a professional who can help tailor a solution to your specific circumstances.

ADDITIONAL NOTES

Common Objections

am often keeping my debate sword sharp on the internet, so I have collected some of the many objections I have seen online regarding polarity for the reader. Some of these are actually quite informative, so pay close attention.

> **"Men**: *Women may say or think they want men to talk about feelings, ask for help, cry, and be vulnerable, but they actually don't. Those typically feminine behaviors will shut down attraction and make a woman disinterested."*

Masculine men may not often show emotion by accessing the feminine side of their minds, but they wouldn't be able to function within society without it.

It's easy for people to assume that men cannot show emotion, expression, or empathy, but this view is overly simplistic.

Scientifically speaking, men lower their testosterone in exchange for estrogen when their baby is about to be born. This shift can lead to heightened emotional sensitivity, which is crucial for optimal survival and bonding.

Across the board, men in long-term relationships tend to have less testosterone than men who are single and dating. This is often because they are required to be more emotionally present to maintain the relationship.

While this data might have a modern bias, I can personally attest that, while women appreciate incredible stoicism and strength in a man, they also want to see the mother, as I call it, present within him.

This is where a man can be more funny, creative, empathetic, and capable of shaping his mission in a way that involves others.

The peak of the female mind within a man is his ability to be loved by all, not just respected. This allows him to achieve an optimal form of competency that inspires the masses to follow him. In this state, he can vulnerably share his story and pull a crowd in to listen.

So yes, women may not want to see all the traits mentioned in this image on a daily basis, but they do want a man to be capable of them, just as a man wants a woman to be **capable** of competency and survival.

> "**Men**: Women need the boundaries of the patriarchy and a purpose in life, which is usually a husband and their children. Absent such structure, they malfunction and destroy civilizations."

This statement might provoke a strong reaction from many women because of its bluntness and apparent ignorance. However, I encourage the reader to consider it from a broader perspective, as I did when I first addressed this idea publicly. My response was as follows:

Our civilization today is heavily yin-dominated, so on a macro level, the statement holds some truth.

We see a scarcity of yang-energy in modern society, reflected in our shift away from the ruggedness of the hunt and forage toward reliance on livestock and agriculture. We prioritize preservation and chase excessive comfort.

In many families, masculine fathers are absent, leaving children to be raised by feminized men or overly masculinized mothers.

It's not about placing blame solely on women but recognizing that humanity as a whole has leaned into yin, or feminine energy, to guide the world. This shift has been especially evident in global trends over the past two decades.

> *"**Men**: Why should I have to be the one who initiates or leads? Relationships should be equal partnerships."*

On a primal level, women instinctively seek a man who can take charge of the physical world, allowing her to focus on nurturing relationships and channeling her feminine energy toward deeper, spiritual connections. The more a woman is consumed by managing the physical world, the less capacity she has to engage with those higher, intuitive aspects of her nature.

From a scientific perspective, women who assume significant power and control in the physical domain—as discussed earlier in this book—may experience elevated testosterone levels. This hormonal shift can subtly disrupt the balance of her femininity, potentially altering her emotional and relational dynamics.

> "**Men:** There is no such thing as a 'gold digger.' Women are naturally expensive, so pick one in your price range and STFU!"

The tribal model is everything. Everything else is a lie. We have not evolved beyond our natural blueprint.

What did men provide back then?

Primarily food and protection.

They urinated along the boundaries of the tribal colony, signaling to opportunistic predators that a dangerous foe resided within, thanks to the high testosterone content in their urine. They also ventured out, hunting strategically with their brotherhood to bring home the primary source of provision.

This provision was biodegradable; money is not. Men shared their excess with the tribe, doing so happily. I'm not advocating socialism, but amassing a surplus of comfort isn't grounded in truth—it breeds weakness and complacency. Life should be a steady rhythm of survival where everyone contributes and remains healthy.

There is no justification for a woman to desire anything beyond safety, food, shelter, water, and a tribe where she can find purpose. She doesn't need to live in poverty today, but attaching a woman's value to a certain price range is a falsehood.

Women should ask themselves this:

If a man possessed the abilities of Jesus but had almost no money, would she reject his courtship despite him being seen as one of the greatest men in the world? If he provided food, shelter, water, community, and his attention, could she not be happy?

> **"Men**: Why is it 'less masculine' to be in touch with my emotions? Isn't being vulnerable actually a strength?"

As a man, it's important to be "in touch with your emotions," but even more important is knowing how and when to express them. Consider this: if a man narrowly avoids being hit by a car, an overly emotional response might look like running home and exclaiming to his wife, "Babe! I almost got hit by a car—can you believe it?" or slipping into a victim mentality.

In contrast, a masculine man might process the experience internally, thinking, "Alright, I dodged that—nice," and move on without feeling the need to share. For some, it might not even register as a significant event—just another moment in the day's challenges.

However, emotions have their rightful place. If a man loses someone close to him, it's entirely appropriate for him to grieve and even cry. While some women may react negatively to such displays of emotion, this is often linked to their own unresolved struggles with a father figure. The key lies in context—knowing when the gravity of a situation warrants an emotional response.

A man also needs emotional attunement to connect with his children. While he can hold firm expectations for them, he must adjust his approach, showing empathy and patience. He cannot interact with his children in the same way he handles grown men at work. At home, a softer, more understanding demeanor is essential for guiding and nurturing them effectively.

> **"Men**: Men are supposed to lead with purpose in the home. You mentioned that women are the primary teachers of purpose, why?"

Both the father and mother play crucial roles in teaching purpose, but no man can fully access his higher power without embracing the feminine side of his mind. Raw masculinity is grounded here on earth, while raw femininity resides in the heavens, far removed from the material world. The blend of these two energies brings us into the lives we live, while also granting us the capacity for spiritual connection.

For women, letting go of control is essential in reaching the shared purpose of a couple. However, the reality is that the man is often away while the children remain with her. Both parents have the ability to speak to and teach purpose, but the mother is naturally attuned to a deeper connection that transcends human comprehension. Those who have felt this connection may interpret it differently, but there is a universal truth: it undeniably exists.

Historically, some indigenous tribes recognized and respected the insights of women with extraordinary abilities—those who could foresee events, contribute as healers, or serve as spiritual guides. These women often held a profound connection to a purpose beyond the physical realm. While men can also access this connection, the feminine intuition equips many women uniquely for this role.

Ultimately, men and women are meant to share the same purpose, but it is the man's role to lead the mission toward that purpose. He is the one who brings it into reality.

> *"**Women**: Why should I have to be softer or more vulnerable? I like being independent and strong."*

Masculine men are drawn to women who can be independent but don't center their identity on independence.

Softness and vulnerability are magnetic to these strong protectors because they ignite a deep, hormonal instinct to provide and protect. It's much like the natural pull a capable man feels when he encounters a young boy lacking competence. He senses that what he possesses—his knowledge and experience—is needed, and he's drawn to share it, helping the boy develop the confidence and skills necessary to navigate the world.

In the same way, a woman's genuine need for a man's masculine energy not only fulfills her but also inspires him to rise further into his masculinity. It's a mutual dynamic that elevates both.

> *"**Women**: Why should he be in charge or lead? I'm just as capable—maybe more so."*

Women today are undoubtedly capable of embodying nearly everything a man can, but that capability doesn't necessarily mean that a woman would—or should—desire to be a man.

Increasingly, I see women striving to embrace both masculine ego and power while simultaneously attempting to hold on to their femininity. However, as illustrated in the earlier example of Leonidas and the 300 Spartans, our energetic focus often requires a trade-off. Leonidas, for instance, might experience a drop in testosterone if he were present at the birth of his child, as his body adjusts hormonally to suit the moment. Similarly, women in positions of power and influence can experience subtle shifts in their thought processes as their hormonal environment becomes more masculine over time.

While society today allows us the freedom to embody whichever roles we choose, we must also acknowledge the health consequences of prolonged reversals in gender dynamics. When women consistently step into male roles, or men into female roles, there's an inevitable toll on hormonal balance and overall well-being.

Anything that boosts testosterone in men tends to enhance their vitality and zest for life. Similarly, women thrive when their estradiol levels are optimized. However, women face a more intricate balancing act due to the risk of estrogen dominance, which remains a prevalent challenge.

> **"Women:** *Men need to be put in their place sometimes, and they often make immature decisions."*

Women often find themselves caught up in a heightened sense of ego, fueled by the validation they receive online through likes, frequent flirtation, and the development of competencies that make them more masculine and self-sufficient.

This inflated ego can manifest as the "adult" within her, which can lead her to assume a position of superiority over her partner. In doing so, she inadvertently brings out the "child" within him— not the joyful, playful child she is meant to awaken, but one that cowers in response to her masculinity. Instead of fostering fun and connection, this dynamic can push the man into behaviors like lying to avoid confrontation or placating her emotions to achieve specific outcomes.

When women operate from a place of judgment and self-righteousness—often stemming from inherently flawed judgment—it tends to do more harm than good. This kind of judgment is better left to a man's brotherhood or mentors, those who can hold him accountable and guide him without undermining his masculinity.

> "**Women:** He has to at least have some land for me to be interested in him, I'm already 33 years old."

Generally, it's okay to want the additional offerings that modern man can provide, but it's important to acknowledge that they are modern and do often take us away from the blueprint.

Provision with the first human beings was simply biodegradable food. Men provided shelter, sustenance, and the tribe brought happiness and connection.

Perceiving any need beyond that isn't natural. Aiming for more is great, but making it a baseline expectation is folly.

One reality is that it's very rare for a man in his early twenties to not be building and to have excess. His earlier twenties are by all accounts his most potent means of reproduction biologically. Men are intended to procreate that early, and are pushing it when they pass 35, and this is even worse for women.

So if the expectation is that a man needs to wait until 35 where many men finally make it, it's a huge biological flaw that is a lived lie.

Living a lie is why we are here today, diseased and lost. We must venture back to the truth or it will only get worse.

So ultimately, yes it's good to aim for more, bad for a woman to expect more than the basics when she is under 35 years old. Her contribution is to multiply his income through inspiration, not to jump in when he's already made it; as that is not only unnatural, but a love story that could have been more profound; a story worth telling.

To me, living a life that is both unnatural, but also not a story worth telling, is not a way to live life.

> **"Men and women**: *Surely not even most people can 'polarize,' because life is complex and nuanced. Some people are just born the way they are."*

I firmly believe that most of us possess the capacity to polarize, and this gives me immense hope for humanity. While some may not be able to—due to age, health conditions, or other factors— the majority of us can. For those individuals, I hope this book inspires a deeper dive into themselves and their untapped potential.

We can cleanse our bodies of heavy metals, as I did. We can work toward balancing our microbiomes, striving for optimal endocrine health through a strong microbial foundation. We can maintain more vibrant relationships by prioritizing our physical health—health that supports mental stability, which is crucial to nurturing those relationships. And we can unite to transform our environment, reducing the toxins we are exposed to daily.

Polarity, then, is the natural result of achieving hormonal equilibrium, which comes from the restoration of nearly every system in the body. This is no simple task, as countless modern-day factors disrupt our systems. For me, it's been a nine-year journey to reach this point at 31, finally feeling grounded in my masculine identity. I can't help but wish I had access to this book when I first began—it would have likely cut this long journey in half, if not more.

> **"Men and women**: It's a huge mistake to vocalize a literal list of "rules" or "boundaries" or whatever to someone you're interested in, whether man or woman... it's weird and distinctly business-like.

Women need to feel safe, and there's no safety without clarity. A lack of clarity leaves a woman on edge, often defensively navigating uncertainty. Defense leads to judgment, and judgment is often the seed of a relationship's demise.

As a man, you must establish what your metaphorical ship is built to do—its mission, its destination, and how her role fits into the journey. This is not optional; it's fundamental. It is not a woman's role to do this.

Women with a masculine focus in their minds often resist this, as it challenges their ability to access deeper vulnerability. They struggle to release control, making it harder for them to accept a clear framework.

In an ideal world, boundaries wouldn't need constant enforcement. But this isn't an ideal world. The pervasive deception, the widespread masculinization of women, and the feminization of men have muddied relational dynamics. Everything now demands a higher level of intentionality and clarity.

Women are not designed to be interviewers, constantly probing and testing. Men must set the stage for them to feel secure, allowing them to relax into their natural softness and sweetness. If a man fails to create this environment early on, women are left with no choice but to adopt a direct and masculine approach—something that should never have been their burden.

> **"Men and women**: A partnership where both are winning is perfectly okay."

It is perfectly okay, but this book isn't about being 'okay.' It's about charting greatness and uncovering raw truth.

Feminine women seek provision only when they need it. Masculine men, on the other hand, seek provision because they have others to protect and provide for, while also fulfilling their drive to overcome challenges and compete with other men.

A society filled with healthy masculine men allows women to focus entirely on the home and tribe, without the need to provide for themselves.

This is where many women lose their way today. They fulfill their need for children, a great husband, tribe, or parental roles by going to work and calling that their purpose. Their most important purpose is in creation and inspiration at home and within the tribe.

The tribal model is fulfilling to every woman.

How did Asa do it?

Understanding people through the thousands I've met during my years in a feminine-leaning career—spanning marketing, service, and customer relations—provided a strong foundation for much of the content in this book. Through my personal experiences and my intense study of health, I've come to realize the profound imbalances that exist in the world. By confronting both my personal flaws and the shortcomings of society, I've found a way to radically transform, physically and mentally, opening doors I never thought possible.

When I combined my life experiences with the skills I gained through my time at Northwest Survival School, I began to repair my body through a wide range of practices. These included dry fasting, mega-dosing microgenderome-positive probiotics, taking large amounts of iodine, grounding in water while basking in sunlight, practicing deep nasal breathing, and most importantly, engaging earnestly in prayer, asking God to heal my body so I could make a meaningful difference in the world.

This marks a basic summary of how I masculinized during the final stages of that segment of my healing journey. It's essential to note, however, that I still faced ups and downs and remained vulnerable to setbacks caused by external circumstances. While it was a significant step forward, one I had fervently prayed for, there was still more work to be done.

As I've healed, I'm realizing I was designed to be a soldier, but debilitating health issues from every angle shaped me into something else. If I ever fully heal, I might become a fighter or, as an example, join a team of men rescuing sex slaves. This book is my way of fighting at this time.

Before, I couldn't imagine becoming that man and relied solely on my intellectual abilities to survive. This book exists because of that path, but every day, I'm moving further from intellectual pursuits and seeking to live more fully in my body; striking a balance between the two.

I'll always help people and likely remain a coach, but everything feels different now. Since reaching this threshold of health and awakening, everything has changed. I want that same transformation for the rest of the world—for those who want to become who they were meant to be.

Readers should understand that their own journey will be unique, but with earnest prayer, there is always hope. Remember, too, that our spiritual journeys are deeply intertwined with our physical bodies. **The bodily experience cannot be overlooked in the pursuit of drawing closer to God if that is what you seek**.

How Polarity Saves the World: Societal Impact

For the following content, please know that I love ALL people. I have friends with vastly different outlooks than mine, and many more who are not 'polarized,' and who have an attraction to alternative sex or hold different views on gender altogether. My intention here is nothing more than to bring clarity to what someone is attracted to and why, and to help uncover solutions for those who want to discover who they could become with optimal psychological and hormonal health.

With all that said, the entire premise of this section of the book is to help people see, from a broad point of view, how achieving optimal health and then fostering optimal polarized relationships can save the world. I ask the reader to have patience with the content provided ahead, as it is necessary in order to get the whole picture.

Blended family dynamics, where traditional gender roles are reversed or less defined, can sometimes appear to work on the surface, but their long-term impact on subsequent generations can be more complex than many realize. When fathers are frequently criticized by mothers, they can inadvertently create archetypes where the child (often a daughter) internalizes the mother's critical role. This can lead to the daughter seeking out future relationships where she holds high standards, often unconsciously mirroring her perception of her father's inadequacy, which can complicate the child's future relational dynamics.

Moreover, while some families manage to maintain a facade of unity, children can often sense that the emotional connection between their parents may not be as solid as it appears. This lack of visible harmony between the mother and father can create a subtle, yet impactful, example for children, teaching them that relational cohesion may not be a priority or even a possibility in adult relationships.

Furthermore, the modern pressures on women to pursue careers, often at the expense of their physical health, are frequently underestimated. Chronic stress, particularly from work, is a major factor that can contribute to the development of conditions like endometriosis, as it disrupts the endocrine system and negatively impacts fertility. Anecdotal evidence from clients and discussions in online groups suggests that women who step away from high-stress careers can experience significant improvements in their health and fertility. In the past, a previous client had benefitted from one of my gut health programs. He had later seen me promoting polarized relationship modeling for optimal hormonal health. This perspective was counter to how he was living, and so he objected to what I was presenting. Surely enough, after trying it out with his lady, they managed to conceive twins after much failure.

When we bring it all together, the systemic degradation of the family unit from many angles sets the stage for much of an individual's identity—an identity that can be shaped into kink-driven sexual dynamics in the search for fulfillment, often without the individual even realizing it.

BDSM Driven By Family Dynamics

Understand that this section generally only looks at more of a psychological role within BDSM. It in no way seeks to eliminate or sidestep the horrors of childhood sexual, physical, and psychological abuses, leading to potentially destructive behaviors later in life. I wish to also recognize that one can be driven toward BDSM simply through physical health problems.

When children grow up without healthy models of masculinity and femininity, they may develop unconscious needs to fill these gaps. This can often lead them to seek out complex relational dynamics, sometimes manifesting in BDSM. The behaviors and desires associated with BDSM are not merely about sexual exploration, but are often deep psychological attempts to address and resolve unmet emotional and psychological needs. These needs can arise from the absence or distortion of healthy parental figures and their role in shaping a child's understanding of gender and relational roles.

The desire to engage in these behaviors can be seen, in some cases, as a means of recreating and resolving the emotional voids left by inadequate or inconsistent modeling of masculinity and femininity in childhood. This unconscious search for balance may drive individuals toward extreme or misdirected ways of fulfilling their psychological needs. Understanding BDSM within this context reveals its connection to deeper psychological processes—often rooted in the struggle to reconcile internalized experiences of lack or neglect during formative years.

Bondage/Discipline (B/D):

Bondage Personal Research

Bondage, when considered from a developmental psychology perspective, can symbolize an unconscious attempt to recreate a sense of safety, containment, and trust that may have been lacking in early life. This is especially true in relation to the maternal figure. For many, bondage mirrors the soothing, protective qualities typically offered by a mother, such as being held or swaddled. If these nurturing experiences were absent or inconsistent, individuals may seek out bondage as a way to fulfill that unmet need for safety. The physical restraint in bondage provides a controlled environment where vulnerability can be experienced, evoking a sense of security and protection.

In cases where childhood experiences involve neglect, emotional abandonment, or overbearing figures, bondage can serve as a tool for rebuilding trust and reestablishing a sense of security. By being bound, individuals can explore vulnerability on their own terms, allowing them to feel cared for and contained in ways that may have been missing earlier in life. The act of submission through bondage, thus, becomes a conscious choice to revisit a state of comfort and safety, offering an opportunity for emotional healing and empowerment.

Throughout my journey in the scene, I found myself craving the attention of my first Domme to such an extent that I experienced genuine overwhelm in her absence. I experienced profound anxiety in the absence of her command and presence. The weeks when I had only spoken to her once were particularly challenging, as she fulfilled two significant voids in my life: my need for a paternal figure and for a lover.

Bondage Personal Experience

I often noticed that people within "the scene," as we called it, carried significant bodily anxiety. While this is largely a matter of physical health in my opinion, many sought external psychological outlets to manage their unease. One approach, from my personal experience, involved surrendering control to a dominant figure within the scene, which provided me with a sense of stability and relief. Interestingly, I hypothesize that seeking external masculine energy might trigger an internal androgenic response, potentially suppressing anxiety. Research supports this, as male hormones, or androgens, are known to play a role in reducing fear and anxiety.

Discipline Personal Research

Discipline is more than just punishment; it's a form of attention and care. A father who disciplines with thoughtfulness communicates that he is invested in his child's well-being and future. Without this dynamic, an adult may unconsciously seek situations wherein discipline becomes a substitute for validation. For those who lacked paternal affirmation in their upbringing, being disciplined can become linked to being noticed, cared for, or even loved.

Healthy masculinity offers protection, order, and stability, with discipline being one of its key expressions. When discipline is missing in formative relationships, the desire for it in adulthood often reflects a deeper need to reconnect with the father figure. It's not so much about punishment as it is about feeling grounded and secure in the presence of authority and care.

Discipline Personal Experience

In the BDSM scene, my main desire was to be dominated as a way to be called out and punished for half-assing things or trying to cover it up. When I told my mom about some of my dreams and fantasies, she changed the way she disciplined me—because, essentially, I was admitting that I found something like that attractive when it came from women. From there, it grew into more than just childhood experiences; it became about a deep need to be caught and put in my place for the concocted illusion of control I had over my mom growing up, which should've been handled by the father role in the first place.

Dominance/Submission (D/S):

Dominance Personal Research

The desire for dominance can often be traced to an individual's need to feel empowered and in control, especially when they may have felt powerless or overlooked in their early years. This isn't necessarily about lacking a father figure but rather about the absence of a balanced dynamic of control, security, or guidance. For some, emotional neglect, inconsistent boundaries, or a lack of guidance from a paternal or authoritative figure can lead them to seek dominance as a way to regain stability and power in relationships.

For others, the drive for dominance stems from a more complex relationship with masculinity itself. Dominance isn't just about control—it's about the ability to lead, protect, and provide structure. If these qualities weren't experienced in their upbringing, especially from male role models, individuals might feel the need to assert these traits to feel grounded. In these cases, dominance often fulfills an unconscious need to restore boundaries and order, filling the gap left by early instability. It can also reflect a desire to overcome the vulnerability that comes from unprotected or unstructured childhood experiences, where a lack of stability could have left them feeling uncertain or exposed.

Dominance Personal Experience

In the later stages of my healing journey, I began exploring domination. A central driver for this was the profound satisfaction of being received by women while maintaining my regular autonomy and being supported by another. Within this framework, I developed a deeper understanding of the natural dynamics between men and women and the dance they share between dominance and submission.

Submission Personal Research

The desire for submission often arises from a range of psychological dynamics, particularly tied to the absence or distortion of healthy role models during childhood. Those who gravitate toward submissive roles in relationships, especially within BDSM contexts, often carry an unconscious need to feel cared for, protected, and guided— qualities that should ideally come from nurturing parental figures. When these qualities are absent, particularly from a mother or father, individuals may develop a subconscious desire to relinquish control in certain areas of their lives. In doing so, they attempt to recreate a sense of safety or seek comfort in the structure and boundaries provided by another.

Submission often symbolizes a form of surrender—not necessarily to control, but as a way to achieve emotional or psychological security that was missing in childhood. Individuals who have lacked consistent affection, guidance, or a balance of firm yet loving discipline may feel compelled to seek out experiences in which someone else assumes responsibility for their well-being.. For some, submission serves as a response to feelings of powerlessness or neglect, offering a way to relieve anxiety about control or uncertainty. In this dynamic, submission isn't a sign of weakness, but a profound desire for balance—something absent during their formative years. It creates a sense of order and comfort, providing an opportunity to surrender in a safe, structured environment where vulnerabilities can be acknowledged and cared for, much like a healthy, protective, and nurturing relationship should offer.

Submission Personal Experience

Submission was a significant part of who I was. There were days when I would obsessively focus on how vulnerable and submissive I could make myself, believing this would attract dominant women. Ironically, it's quite funny how this dynamic works exceptionally well for women with dominant men, but is not nearly as effective for submissive men with dominant women. Dominant women often still have a strong desire for their submissive male partners to be capable of achieving and accomplishing things, much like any dominant man would.

There's even a niche corner of the internet where dominant women actively seek men with wealth and power who are willing to submit to them. However, such 'alpha subs'—men who possess significant resources while maintaining a relatively masculine demeanor—are rare, though they do exist. I fell more into the category of an alpha sub in the sense that I was highly capable and could accomplish a great deal, but I lacked the financial resources that some dominant women sought.

Sadism/Masochism (S/M):

Sadism Personal Research

Sadism, psychologically, can be rooted in unresolved issues around power and control, often shaped by dysfunctional or imbalanced parental relationships. When a child lacks a clear, healthy model of assertiveness or leadership—typically modeled by a strong, authoritative father figure—they may turn to sadistic behaviors as a way to regain control, assert dominance, or cope with past feelings of powerlessness. The desire to inflict pain or humiliation on others often stems from a deep need to feel superior, compensating for emotional neglect or mistreatment. This behavior isn't necessarily about cruelty for its own sake but rather about testing boundaries, asserting authority, and re-establishing self-worth in environments where they may have felt vulnerable or weak during childhood.

Sadism in the context of BDSM or relationships can reflect a desire to express power in a controlled and structured way. It often serves as an outlet for unresolved frustrations, the need for recognition, or a way to balance perceived inadequacies. For some, sadism can intertwine with elements of performance and identity, enabling them to express emotions or experiences they may not be able to in everyday life. The root of sadistic behavior can often be traced to a complex mix of unmet emotional needs, especially the absence of a firm, assertive figure during critical developmental periods. This lack of leadership may lead to the enactment of power and control as a means of self-affirmation. However, just as with any extreme expression of desire, a careful and conscious approach is required to prevent the destructive consequences of unresolved emotional pain.

Sadism Personal Experience

Sadism has probably been the most complex aspect of BDSM for me. During the worst phases of my gastrointestinal health, I noticed my desires for sadism growing stronger and stronger. However, during periods when I exclusively consumed raw meat, those desires almost completely vanished. Interestingly, I also found that fasting helped reduce these urges, though not as effectively as the raw meat diet. When I first started eating an all-raw meat diet in 2018, I experienced what felt like a profound metabolic shift—almost like a spiritual transformation. It gave me a sense of feeling lifted above my fleshly desires and free from the pull of justifiable wrath or the need for exacting justice against those who had done unspeakable things. Instead, I could look at such individuals and see who they were before their paths were, at times in brutal ways, altered and they came to believe in the lies or deep wounds that shaped their actions.

The most perplexing part is that an all-cooked meat diet had the opposite effect—it seemed to keep the urges alive. Yet, switching to all-raw meat completely eradicated them. The only explanation I can think of is the difference in how raw versus cooked meat impacts the body on a chemical level. Perhaps it has to do with B vitamins being water-soluble and losing their bioavailability when cooked, or maybe it involves how raw meat interacts with gut microbes compared to cooked meat.

Over the last few years, my desires for sadism have significantly diminished. They now feel much more normalized, aligning with activities like hunting, MMA, or addressing injustices. I suspect that factors such as oxalates, fungi, and heavy metals may contribute to the development of sadistic tendencies by potentially influencing neurotransmitters. My belief stems from the observation that eating raw meat still affects my mood and curbs any inclination toward sadism, though not as strongly as it did when I first began the diet.

From the initial phase of eating raw meat, I maintained a childlike wonder, where even something as simple as a blade of grass seemed beautiful and fascinating. However, I've never fully recovered that sense of clarity and lightness since deviating from that diet. This leads me to theorize that adaptive system functions—such as opportunistic microbes expanding their footholds and adapting to the environment the raw meat created—might be responsible for the diminished impact of the diet over time.

Please note that I do not advocate for the average person to consume raw meat, and that I personally haven't mastered how to eat it in the most effective way for my own body.

Masochism Personal Research

Masochism can often be understood as a coping mechanism linked to unresolved psychological and emotional conflicts, particularly those shaped by early childhood experiences. It frequently stems from a history of abuse, neglect, or a lack of nurturing and protective care, which should have come from primary caregivers, typically the mother or father. The desire to endure pain or humiliation in the context of masochism can reflect a need for validation, attention, or a sense of control in a world where the individual may have felt powerless, insignificant, or unloved. In this case, the need for punishment may serve as a way to recreate past experiences where affection or attention was tied to suffering or sacrifice, such as in environments where love was shown only in response to hardship or when emotional needs were ignored.

The masochistic tendency to seek pain or humiliation can also be connected to a distorted sense of self-worth. If a child grows up in an environment where approval or affection appears conditional on suffering or submission, they may come to believe that pain is an integral part of receiving care or love. As an adult, this belief can manifest in situations where the person seeks to "earn" affection or attention through self-inflicted suffering or degradation. In this sense, masochism can be seen as an ingrained but misguided attempt to feel valued or acknowledged, even if it means enduring discomfort or harm. Psychological theories often point to the influence of childhood attachments and parental behaviors—particularly neglect or emotional unavailability—on the development of these adult desires. In the realm of BDSM or similar relational dynamics, masochism may serve not only as a form of emotional release but also as a way to create order out of chaotic emotional experiences, helping the individual manage them in a controlled and structured environment.

Masochism Personal Experience

My personal drivers for masochism were unique. Many people around me in the BDSM world who identified as submissives had a desire for masochism, while others had little to no interest. I wasn't drawn to the pain itself but was deeply intrigued by the intensity, the challenge, and the dynamic of earning forgiveness through the ordeal. The best way I could describe it was as "mental/emotional masochism," though, in reality, what I was seeking was masculine discipline from women. For me, masochism was not about pain, it was about correction, discipline and redemption.

Role of Masculinity and Femininity

Masculine Energy: Traditionally, masculinity offers protection, provision, and structure. When this is absent or inconsistent, individuals may seek dominance or authority figures to fill the void or may become overly dominant themselves as a defense mechanism.

Feminine Energy: Feminine role models or mothers bring nurturing, emotional safety, and softness. If these elements are lacking, individuals may seek submission or masochism as a way to receive the care or emotional release they didn't get during childhood.

Concluding BDSM

Personally, the BDSM scene in some ways was a means for me to find answers. On a spiritual level, however, I wouldn't suggest that this justifies others jumping in to find theirs. Thankfully, I've discovered alternative methods for helping people break free from those cycles without delving into the world of alternative sexuality. My program, *Pass the Torch*, is one of those methods and works strongly when it's done right. I couldn't get it off the ground as its own startup, though, because I wasn't able to sell people on how important it is or how effective it can be. With this book, I'm hoping to make the case more clearly, so people will seek me or the mentors I've trained, to help them find their way out.

The psychological points I've touched on above are just a simple way to break down the issue. There are deeper physical factors at play that can influence a person's desire to get into BDSM. Things like hormonal imbalances, gut health issues, mineral deficiencies, and tragically, brutal childhood physical and sexual trauma, all tie into emotional and psychological needs, creating a complicated mix of reasons behind these behaviors. It's not something that can be explained fully with just a few examples. Each of these factors plays a role in shaping why someone might be drawn to BDSM. The way the body and mind interact shows just how deep this issue runs. Understanding the physical side would add another important layer to why some people are attracted to these dynamics.

One final point I want to emphasize is that leaving this space is far from easy. I know many individuals who attempt to leave, but regardless of their efforts, their desires remain potent, often overshadowing other natural inclinations that would lead them toward love-based intimacy exclusively. If someone identifies as dominant and transitions into a coaching business while distancing themselves from BDSM, it is not comparable to a man needing to completely alter his gut microbiome, eliminate heavy metals, and address parental voids in an attempt to be the only exception he recognizes. Every reality check that crossed my mind when looking at how everyone else is experiencing this situation was telling me that I wasn't going to make it. Even as I write this book, and if I deviate from my usual path with health, and God, there are brief openings available for me to dive back in, albeit far more diminished and less attractive on every level. *I once encountered a dominatrix who identified as one due to her autistic traits, characterized by a spiritual detachment and an emphasis on cold sadism. She later shared with me that she had become a vanilla house wife after killing off fungus in her body, going low oxalate with diet, and doing chelation therapy.*

Fighting these desires can be a very lonely battle for the majority, and while I had my mother and sister, it still felt so lonely. I wasn't receiving any answers from therapists, natural or medical doctors, and certainly not from anyone within the scene. So I willfully decided to blaze my own trail to healing, praying the entire time. Although I went to church with my family, I never truly felt or connected with God until that one dry fast, but I held onto the belief that someone was watching over me. Now I find myself at the finish line, surrounded by a world polluted by nnEMFs, heavy metals, and sugar traps that could lead to bacterial infections for me (a long story in itself). It feels particularly challenging as society increasingly embraces, even celebrates, the very things I've been striving so hard to resist and escape from. To each their own, but the majority of the world of BDSM is driven by poor health, dysfunction and past abuse... I will take that to my grave.

LGBTQ+ Driven by Family Dynamics

The following is by no means exhaustive and is merely meant to add weight to the argument in favor of polarity. This topic alone requires an entire book to fully explore the connections between psychology and physiology, and how they intersect to affect identity.

"64% of heterosexual adults experienced at least one adverse childhood experience (ACE), with 26% experiencing three or more ACEs. **Among sexual minority adults, 83% had at least one ACE, and 52% had three or more ACEs.**"

(***doi:***10.1001/jamapsychiatry.2022.0001).

An adverse childhood experience (ACE) is often defined as a trauma that occurs during a person's formative years. It's commonly believed that adverse sexual attractions or fantasies stem directly from such trauma, yet many people argue they've experienced no significant trauma and still harbor these attractions. In my case, I became drawn to women dominating me beginning around the age of 12, primarily due to the impact of molestation. However, the real anchor for this pattern was a deeper wound tied to the absence of a strong father role. It's crucial to recognize that even voids in childhood—not necessarily classified as ACEs—can significantly influence identity and preferences in relationships.

If we take the findings of the cited study and combine them with the concept of parental role dysfunction—such as a mother focusing too much on masculine traits or a father with a hard focus on feminine ones—it could shed light on why certain individuals are attracted to what they are. While these parental role imbalances don't necessarily lead to ACEs, they could explain much about the attraction patterns in many people.

The Father: For individuals who identify as transgender or gender non-conforming, the lack of a solid, positive male figure in their upbringing can influence their relationship with masculinity. A father wound, in which a child grows up with an emotionally unavailable or absent father, can lead to confusion or dissatisfaction with traditional gender roles. As a result, some individuals may explore non-binary or gender-fluid identities in an effort to transcend to re-acquire the masculine within.

One example can be men I've encountered who have accomplished much in life but are deeply wounded by women, inadvertently becoming more focused on boys. His primal drive to impart knowledge and raise young men capable of handling life may become entangled with his sexual identity. Similarly, the boys may so intensely seek masculine guidance that they end up making the relationship sexual. From the sample pool of individuals I've worked with, it's common to find that men—often mentally stuck as boys and needing to be in that mindset to receive deeply—are seeking to receive from men, highly prevalently within the *Manifestor* core archetype.

The Mother: When a person struggles with their gender identity, particularly in a way that challenges societal norms, it often traces back to the mother's influence. If a child grows up with a mother who is emotionally unavailable, neglectful, or overly controlling, it can deeply affect their sense of femininity or gender expectations. A mother wound like this can cause confusion, making it difficult for the child to feel comfortable in the roles traditionally assigned to women. This emotional disconnect can lead some individuals to explore gender identities that feel more authentic to them, such as non-binary or transgender, as they break free from restrictive norms and seek a truer expression of self. The lack of nurturing from a mother figure can thus shape the journey toward gender identity outside conventional boundaries.

Many men have approached me after I shared my journey of moving beyond BDSM to embrace a fulfilling, vanilla relationship with a feminine woman. A significant number of them either experienced bisexual thoughts or identified as being homosexual. Almost all of them described having a mother who was overly involved in their lives, often due to the father being absent or sidelined. They expressed deep shame about their attractions and sought my perspective. While some reported shifts toward being more attracted to women, this was not universal. Those with specific ACEs, such as molestation, often seemed to have a stronger neurological attachment to the sexual dynamics they had experienced. Interestingly, some shared personal accounts of changes in their attractions or outlook after implementing dietary adjustments. These observations remain anecdotal and are not medically verified.

To clarify, I do not perform 'conversion therapy' or treat psychological or medical conditions. My focus is on supporting individuals through a whole-body wellness approach, helping them explore and achieve their personal goals. All guidance I provide is educational, based on my own experiences and 9+ years of study.

Gender identity is deeply complex, and I've observed that beyond trauma, adverse living environments like jail or rats in a rat cage, parental dysfunction, and metabolic and biochemical pathways can significantly influence one's attraction to the same sex. Hormonal imbalances, neurotransmitter irregularities, and even gut microbiome disruptions can alter the brain's wiring and emotional responses, which may lead to same-sex attraction, irrespective of early life experiences. These biological factors shape desires and perceptions in ways that aren't always tied to emotional or psychological wounds. Often, it's a blend of genetics, hormones, system disturbances like microbes or heavy metals, and environmental triggers that mold someone's identity, and no two experiences are identical.

Generational Illness

When parents suffer from poor physical health, their psychological well-being is inevitably impacted. This issue lies at the heart of most of our problems today, tracing back to the beginning of mankind, where dysfunctional parental figures continue the cycle of abuse due to the powerful effects of poor health on their hormonal and psychological health.

It was during my entry into the world of the carnivore diet that I realized how strongly our so-called 'sinful nature' is influenced by what we eat. I observed hundreds of people become more open-minded about changing their political or religious views after a few months on the diet. This led me to dive deeper into the chemical mechanisms behind this shift.

Candida, the systemic fungus I was born with, produces a metabolite called acetaldehyde after metabolizing glucose in our system. Anatomically, Candida can colonize many areas of the body, particularly the entire gastrointestinal tract (the gut). The body produces neurotransmitters—signaling hormones that are susceptible to acetaldehyde. Around 95% of serotonin, a neurotransmitter, is produced in the gut. When serotonin is disrupted, it can lead to poor regulation of acetylcholine, another neurotransmitter. I view acetylcholine as a "female neurotransmitter," as it plays a key role in memory retention and emotional regulation.

When serotonin is obstructed, it triggers a hormonal cascade that impacts digestive motility, potentially leaving toxic stool to stagnate in the intestine. This in turn can lead to an imbalance in acetylcholine in the brain. Without proper regulation, acetylcholine contributes to what I call 'subconscious brain fog'—a state that makes it difficult for individuals to remain open-minded. Often, this manifests as a preference for comfortable lies over uncomfortable truths.

Candida, as a fungus, has likely been present in the human digestive system for millennia. I wonder if it has always been there—who can say? Beyond Candida, numerous other eukaryotic organisms like parasites and molds can affect neurotransmitters, ensuring their own survival. I suspect that sex addiction, and our often obsessive relationship with sex, may be driven by microbes manipulating our neurotransmitters to guarantee their survival and propagation.

Since the dawn of agriculture, it seems plausible that we introduced nutritional imbalances that allowed yeasts, molds, and parasites to interfere with our hormonal health—because they primarily proliferate off of excess glucose in the system—supporting their ongoing proliferation across generations through dissemination. This theory became more clear to me after I first tried raw meat, which had a feeling of a spiritually cleansing effect on me. It made me feel oddly sinless, allowing me to see past my past trauma. Instead of reacting in righteous indignation toward the woman who molested me, I was able to reflect on what had happened to her and what led her to that point.

At the root of much of the abuse we see in the world lies poor neurotransmitter health. It's this imbalance that perpetuates the cycle of dysfunction, especially among parents who pass on these unresolved emotional and hormonal struggles to the next generation.

World Atrocities

One of my greatest, though often unspoken, ambitions is to vastly reduce the demand for the sex slave trade and the pornography industry.

I believe that when humanity truly absorbs the points I discuss here in this book, my hope is that the desire to exploit others will decrease.

The world's problems are numerous: drug trafficking, the constant demand for sex and pornography, the resulting tragedy of abortion, religious wars, and the persistent destruction of the earth's resources.

However, I believe that when the human body is returned to its original blueprint, wrongdoing will become nearly impossible, as harmful desires would largely fade away. The stronger and more resilient the human system, the less dis-ease will manifest. And with less dis-ease comes more fulfilled and happier lives, focused on the basics: family, food, water, shelter, and the pursuit of a higher calling.

The purpose of this book isn't simply to sell the idea of polarized relationships, but to show that these dynamics existed in harmony before societal health became compromised. With radiant feminine women and powerful masculine men, we can build a world where the atrocities mentioned above no longer hold sway.

The Yin & Yang Pendulum

The symbol of the Yin & Yang, I believe, is an unusually accurate way of describing the ideal balance of life in the world.

In our not-so-distant history, we were burning women on stakes, cutting hands off for theft, or sending boys deemed 'too aggressive' and 'incorrigible' to insane asylums where castration was a means of suppressing the aggression to make them more pliable. This, on a macroscopic level, would be considered actions made within an era widely dominated by 'yang energy.' Authority reigned supreme, and a heavy fist came down over those who defied the structure.

Within short order, as society believed we had advanced beyond this mindset, the pendulum swung steadily to the yin, where 'open-mindedness' and more of a soft touch for therapies became pronounced. A progression of a deeper understanding of human psychology came into play, and a relative balance was forming. Though somehow, very quickly, the pendulum seems to have swung so strongly into the yin that necessary traditional structures have been either eased or completely removed.

An example is the topic just discussed regarding LGBTQ and BDSM. The yin gives way for a kind of open-mindedness that can be good on one end, but for as the pendulum swings further, we can end up at a place where allowing people to express themselves leads to this mentality being taught to children; enough to actually push it on them and potentially even expect it. I am not against people expressing how they feel and having the freedom to do this, but we do need to acknowledge where this expression may be rooted in serious problems related to dis-ease. We can't go about saying loudly that this mentality is healthy and that everyone should be open to it. This is where the yin brings too much irrational thought, where it needs to be centered by the yang.

Letting go of foundational structures that keep the yin from expanding too far has gotten us here, where indulgence of various pleasures such as foods, pornography, social media, and fleeting emotional validation has overridden the natural balance, leading to a state where discipline, resilience, and deeper fulfillment are often sacrificed for momentary gratification.

This subject alone requires its own book to fully define, but I do hope the reader understand from this section of the book just how far we've swung into the yin, and need to balance back with a little more of the yang.

Need Drives Purpose

Men who go through life perceiving that their contribution is small, or generally not needed, will struggle to attach themselves to a purpose. I have been seeing this a lot more now since merging polarized relationship modeling into my 1:1 work, and the implications of this are much greater than one may think.

When men lack having a mission to complete on the way to achieving their purpose (definitions for how I define 'mission' and 'purpose' can be found under the Loose Terms and Definitions section of the book), they can devolve into focusing on self-pleasure, and potentially take this pleasure seeking to a level of depravity; a kind of depravity—when accompanied with power—that could strip the freedom of another innocent person all to pleasure themselves. This is not exclusively reserved to men, but men are heavily affected by this vicious cycle today.

For both sexes, the constantly rising bar for dopamine and thrill-seeking can lead people to try new things that can grow into something very dark, provided their bodily health drives much of the desire for it. Meaning, I believe parasites and fungi primarily drive—via a weakened bodily terrain—much of the depravity we see today, because sexual dissemination into another host would be highly desirable for them. The darkness and depravity I speak of, could be something like the sex slave trade, where innocents are taken and exploited for the momentary pleasures of others with power and an insatiable need for more.

My overarching point with this section of the book is that society needs to be structured in a way that the vast majority of both men and women have something meaningful in their lives to focus on, but to also make men feel more needed. Yes, men make up the vast majority of blue collar workers and other industries, but the times are shifting into a major imbalance with women seeking the same as men as far as work competency is concerned. This is equivalent to women partaking on the hunt just as men do, all while inadvertently invalidating men. When women feel satisfied financially and don't genuinely need men, any romantic endeavors really just become an accessory for her. She can justify all she wants about how much she needs a man for other things, but a woman with vast wealth can pay another man to get everything she needs done. This power exchange strips women of a greater form of vulnerability and trust of men, and of men their ability to feel valued as a strong leader.

Yes, women can have a thriving business while remaining feminine, but her romantic partner is never going to meet his highest potential, and nor will she if the polarities don't unite as the blueprint is intended, which is centered in the wild. Women are best suited to focus on supporting her husband's mission for their shared purpose, and to then nurture children whilst uplifting the tribe through expression. The vast majority of his time spent out on the hunt can be very hard, and that is what men are designed for, so when he arrives back in the tribe, his soft and sweet wife will seem like a reward greater than the accolades granted from bringing back a kill.

Men need something to focus on, and if women can provide for themselves, we invalidate men; we invalidate true masculinity in its raw and fully intended form. Women can survive on their own, but they are not designed to do so perpetually and comfortably. The less women need men, the worse our societal situation gets with more and more depravity forming. So I humbly ask the reader to consider this perspective heavily in how they perceive reality after reading this book. Adopting this perspective, albeit hard to do due to our current societal structure, is one way someone can contribute to positively shaping the world for the better.

We were never supposed to deviate from the blueprint.

Concluding How Polarity Saves the World: Societal Impact

It's not necessary for everyone to eat raw meat or follow a strict carnivore diet. What is essential, however, is that every person must find a way to address their physical and mental health issues and not use them as an excuse for abusive or imbalanced behavior. I don't believe anyone should be forced to eat in a specific way or conform to a single approach. But we must be more serious in recognizing how deeply damaging it is to society when even one person deviates from an optimal state of health.

We need to raise the standard for hormonal health to expect people to want to reach for polarity. If someone is not embodying the traits of a polarized masculine man or a feminine woman, it signals clear imbalance. Once we set that expectation, everything else will follow. People will then naturally strive to become radiant women and emanating men.

It's not to suggest that a *Manifestor* man shouldn't be acknowledged for his talent in creating comedy, or that a *Warrioress* can't be recognized for her ability to guide men in becoming better leaders.

Similarly, individuals who have reached a certain age and feel they can't turn back time shouldn't be seen as lesser; each has their unique strengths and contributions. However, it's important to acknowledge where imbalances exist so that each individual has the opportunity to strive toward higher potential and discover their best self; so that we can stop the cycle and renew hope for following generations.

Under Generational Illness I mentioned that neurotransmitters like serotonin and acetylcholine work together to abate what I call 'subconscious brain fog.' Furthermore, I submit that when the mind opens chemically like this, it can shift deeply held beliefs—whether religious or political. The key lies in accessing the **inner child**, which allows us to **receive** and embody the changes we desire. Children are designed to absorb new information and learn. It is through accessing the female sides of our mind (the child), we can integrate what we unconciously seek to fulfill for full integration.

Through the right balance of neurotransmitters, we can tap into transformative potential, not just intellectually, but on a deeper, more holistic level.

If the reader wants to make immense changes in their life, they must open up their heart and mind on both an intentional psychological level while attributing much of their mental health performance to great physical health.

A Message to the Lost

The journey into identifying our inner demons can become a transformative path to enlightenment and healing.

Without the struggles posed by these darker aspects, I might have settled for a life of superficial success, perhaps marked by material wealth, yet lacking depth and purpose. It's through grappling with these internal challenges that I've found the drive to heal myself and guide others toward their own growth.

The trials imposed by our inner demons can often compel us to surmount metaphorical mountains we might not have dared to climb otherwise. Spiritually, the struggles have enriched my life far more than a "perfect" existence ever could. Facing these challenges with intention—understanding why we are drawn to certain destructive tendencies and seeking to outgrow them—is the key to unlocking deeper fulfillment.

True liberation from what ails us today begins with confronting the truth head-on. By understanding the nature of our inner demons, we dismantle fear and reclaim power over our minds. This process grants freedom of thought, enabling us to gradually let go of lingering untruths. Over time, as we evolve, we no longer find joy in the things which once captivated us. They become like training wheels we've outgrown, unnecessary for our forward journey.

Contrary to the belief that human growth necessitates sin or fallibility, our purpose here may be to overcome these darker aspects. Each of us has inner demons to confront. Embracing this challenge is not only part of the human experience but also central to our evolution into freer, more enlightened, whole, and loving humans.

A thought I wanted to add is that a friend of mine, Brian Kuenning, shared an interesting insight. He hypothesizes that the snake in the Garden of Eden actually represents the human gut. This connects with my thoughts on the gut potentially being the root of all sin. When we finally ascend to gain mastery over our gastrointestinal health, we may no longer be susceptible to opportunisti c microbes that act as vessels for more malefic activity. It is also possible that there is no spiritual nature to the gut and that a mesh of parasites and fungi control our neurotransmitters, leading us to destructive, sinful behaviors. Either way, it makes one wonder if we are meant to have the health that keeps us in this cycle, or we are supposed to conquer it.

Overall Conclusion

Through this book, I hope we can gain a clearer understanding of how the various disruptions to our health today negatively affect our relationships. Perhaps there are no truly "evil" people—just those corrupted by dis-ease and various abuses.

When our gut health suffers, neurotransmitter imbalances follow, often leading to mental health struggles that cause us to lose touch with who we really are. Inflammation typically tags along, raising cortisol levels that can stay elevated, suppressing sex hormones over time. This cascade effect impacts our identities and the relationships we try to build.

Health should be the baseline expectation in every relationship.

As we've seen, many people leave relationships after improving their health, as they outgrow the version of themselves tied to that relationship. But it's not always as simple as it seems. For example, women stuck in a constant state of fight-or-flight with excessive sympathetic nervous system dominance may find peace and balance once their health improves. This shift allows them to embrace their femininity, becoming more attuned to their female hormones, and changing how they see themselves and who they're attracted to.

Health changes deeply influence attraction, which is one reason why women often shift partners after improving their health.

Equally important are the roles of parents or anyone who can truly capture the heart of a child. These figures become integrated into our identities in ways that often go unnoticed. Some, like my mother, have a remarkable ability to take the good and leave the bad, adapting by integrating positive examples from those around them. Much of this resilience comes from patterns of openness and receptivity. That said, I've learned that physical health plays a crucial role in how trauma forms and shapes our lives. Some of us may be genetically fortunate or spiritually resilient, allowing us to process trauma more easily.

One final thought: If we had no parasites, no fungal overgrowth, no nnEMF exposure, no toxic water, no heavy metals attached to receptor sites, no history of antibiotics or chemical injections, and no generational trauma—what would that version of us look like? That's the question I ask myself every day. It's the vision I hold onto as I push forward.

Join me, and let's make men masculine and women feminine again!

Contact

For business inquiries and permissions, contact:

Asa Santiago

917 W Grand Ave. #353

Grover Beach, CA 93433